Contents

Body Systems

The separate body systems combine to enable an individual to perform.

Nervous system

The nervous system takes messages to the brain, so that the brain can decide what to do. The brain then sends its messages on to the muscular system.

Respiratory system

Muscles need oxygen. This is supplied by the respiratory system.

Muscular system

When the muscles receive a signal from the brain they contract.

Circulatory system

Oxygen in the lungs is transferred into the blood of the circulatory system. Once in the blood, it is pumped to the muscles by the heart.

Skeletal system

When the muscles contract they pull on the bones of the skeletal system to create movement.

Hormonal system

The blood also contains hormones from the hormonal system. These help to release energy and fuel from food.

Digestive and excretory system

Food is processed in the digestive system.

All the separate body systems combine together when we take part in sport. Athletes and players can improve their performance through training.

See also The World of Sport Examined Pages **8-39**

The Skeletal System

■ What does the skeleton do?

List the four functions of the skeleton. Then fill in the missing words.

1. ....

      Delicate .... need protection.

      a. The skull protects the ....

      b. The .... protects the spinal cord.

      c. The .... protects the ....

         and the ....

2. ....

      The body needs a ....

      a. This holds the .... in place.

      b. It provides .... for the ....

3. ....

      .... act on bone to cause ....

      a. The skeleton is .... which allows a ....

         ....

      b. Different .... allow ....

         of ....

4. ....

      Red and white ....

      are produced in the .... and other minerals

      are stored in the body.

■ The vertebral column

Complete the sentences using the bank of words below.

The vertebral or .... column is made up of ....

.... Between each is a layer of cartilage which acts as a ....

.... This structure allows .... movement.

33	spinal	vertebra	wide ranging	shock absorber

■ How do bones grow?

Complete the sentences using the bank of words below.

In the embryo, most of the skeleton is made of .... As a baby grows

into childhood and adulthood this changes to .... This process is known

as .... Mature bone contains .... to give hardness

and .... fibres to make it strong and light.

bone	ossification	collagen	calcium	cartilage

© Andy Sibson Published by Thomas Nelson and Sons Ltd. 1997

See also The World of Sport Examined Pages **10-13**  5

The Skeletal System

■ Types of bone

1. There are four different types of bone. Draw an example of each in the boxes below.
2. Give the name of the type of bone and the example you have chosen, and briefly describe what it does.

Type of bone: ....

Example: ....

What it does: ....

....

....

Type of bone: ....

Example: ....

What it does: ....

....

....

Type of bone: ....

Example: ....

What it does: ....

....

....

Type of bone: ....

Example: ....

What it does: ....

....

....

6

See also The World of Sport Examined Page **11**

The Skeletal System

■ The bones in our body

1. Label the skeleton. Write the common names in brackets.
2. Colour the bones of the axial skeleton.
3. Colour the bones of the appendicular skeleton in a different colour.
4. Label the diagram of the vertebral column.

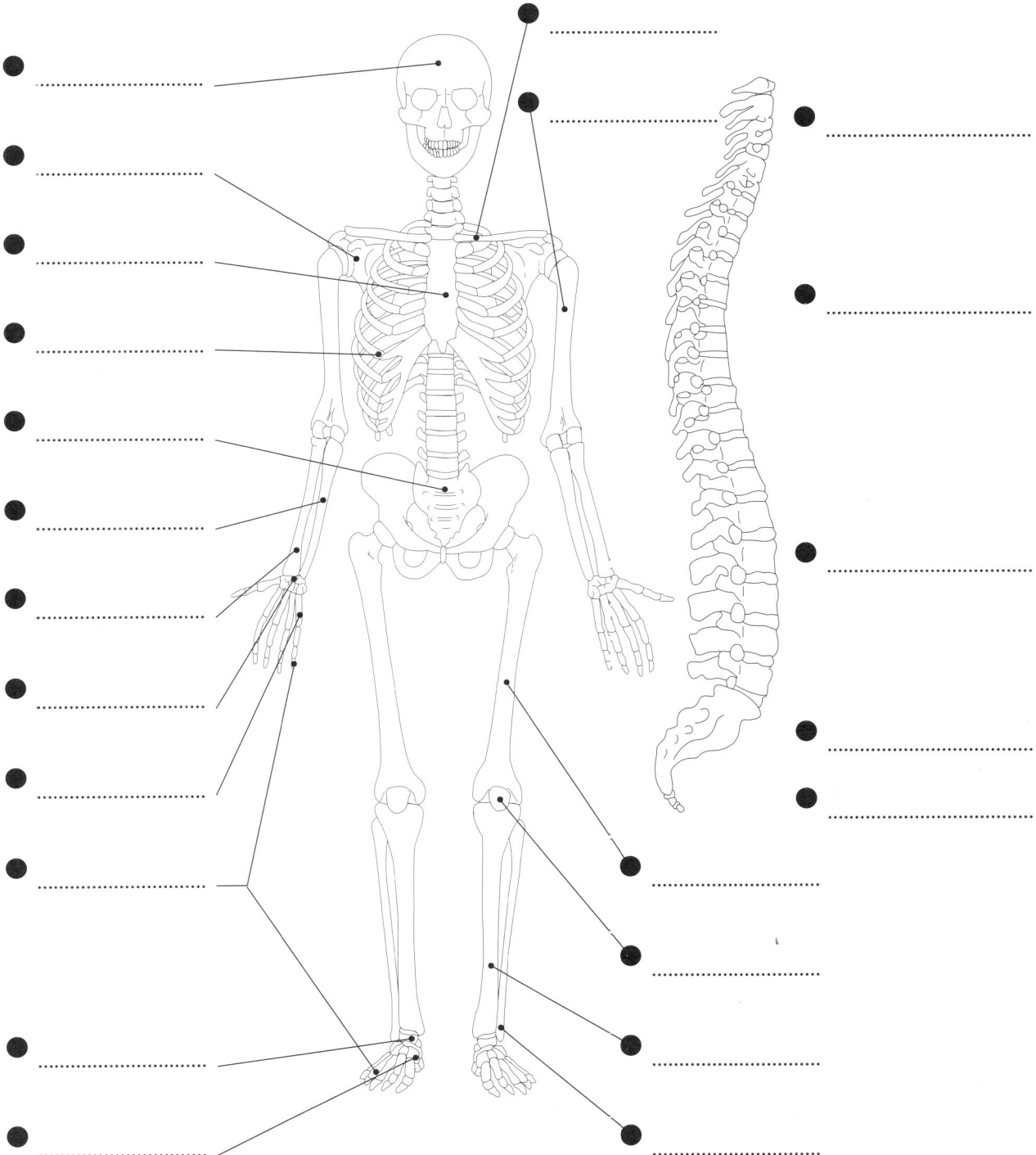

The Skeletal System

■ Joints and movement

The hip joint

1. Label the diagram below.
2. Colour the diagram using a different colour for each component.

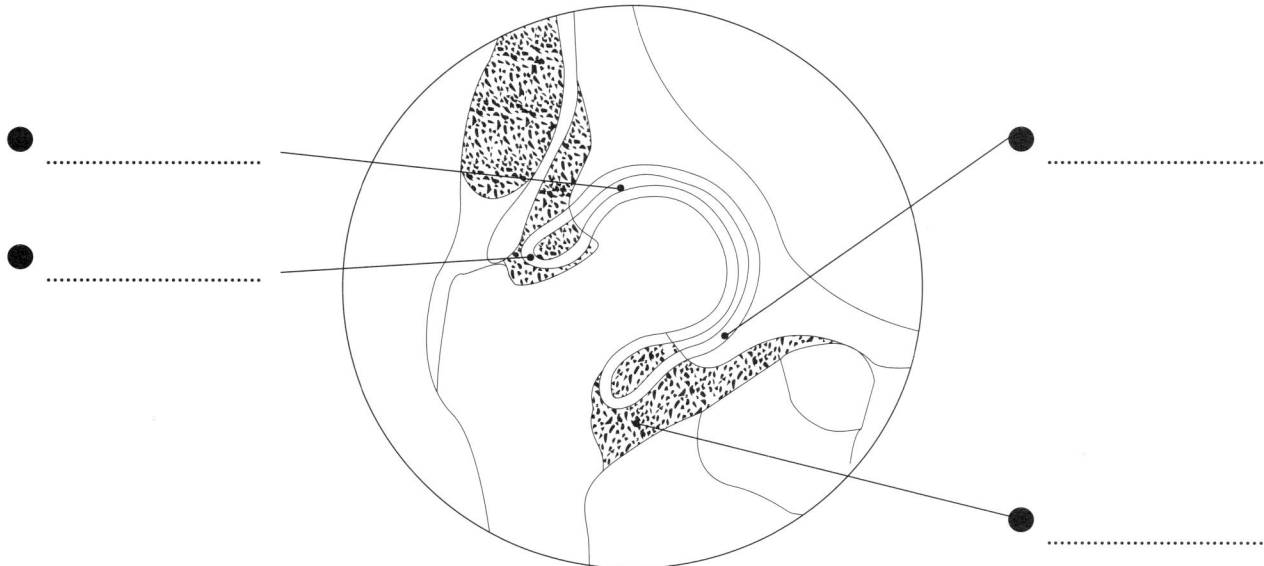

Types of movement at joints

Label the diagrams showing the types of movement most often used when performing.

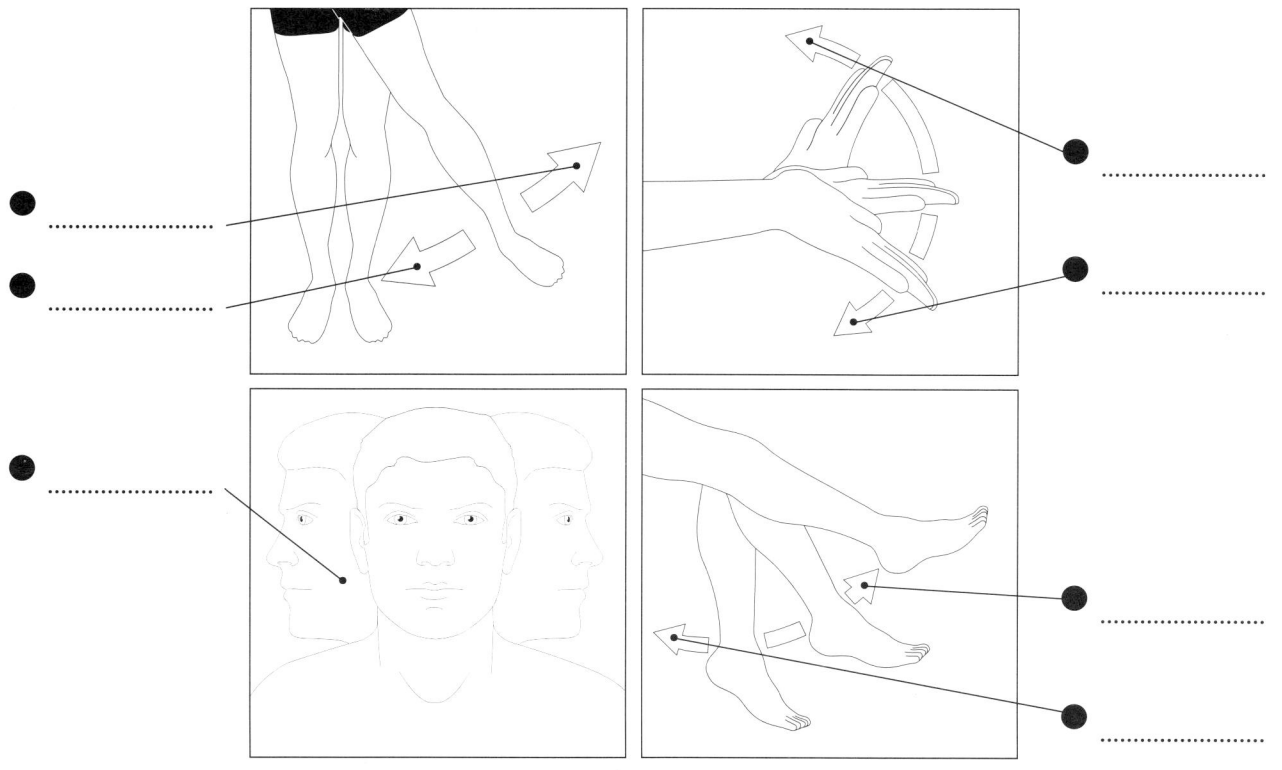

See also The World of Sport Examined Pages **14-16**

© Andy Sibson Published by Thomas Nelson and Sons Ltd. 1997

A. The Skeletal System

■ Types of joint

1. Look at each type of synovial joint shown below.
2. Name each type of synovial joint.
3. Note one example of each within the body.
4. Describe what each one does.
   The first one has been done for you.

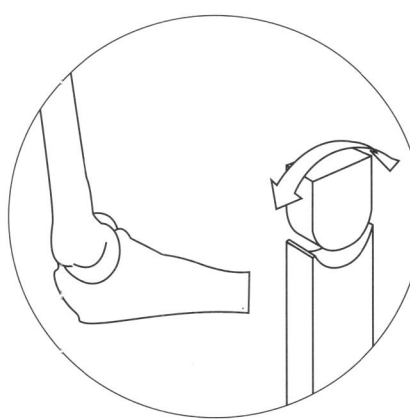

Name: Hinge joint

Example: Elbow

What it does: Moves in one plane only.
Movement is limited by the shape of the bones and the
strong ligaments.

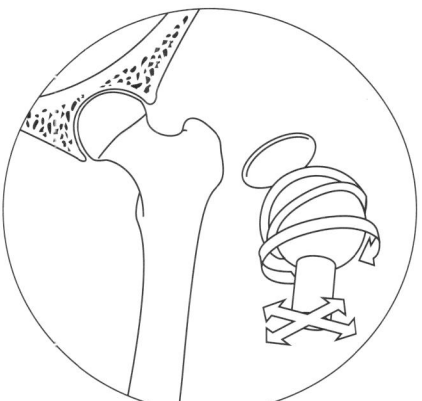

Name: ....

Example: ....

What it does: ....

....

....

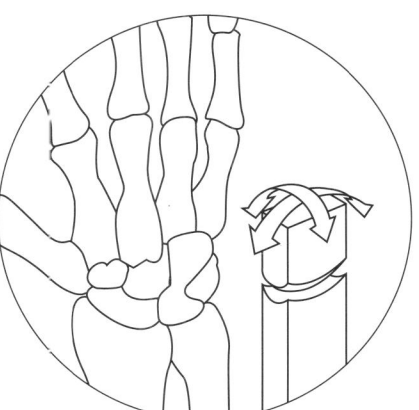

Name: ....

Example: ....

What it does: ....

....

....

See also The World of Sport Examined Page **15**

B. The Skeletal System

■ Types of joint

1. Look at each type of synovial joint shown below.
2. Name each type of joint.
3. Note one example of each within the body.
4. Describe what each one does.

Name: ....

Example: ....

What it does: ....

....

....

Name: ....

Example: ....

What it does: ....

....

....

Name: ....

Example: ....

What it does: ....

....

....

10

See also The World of Sport Examined Page **15**

© Andy Sibson Published by Thomas Nelson and Sons Ltd. 1997

The Muscular System

■ The muscles in our body

1. Label the diagram as indicated.
2. Shade each muscle with a different colour.

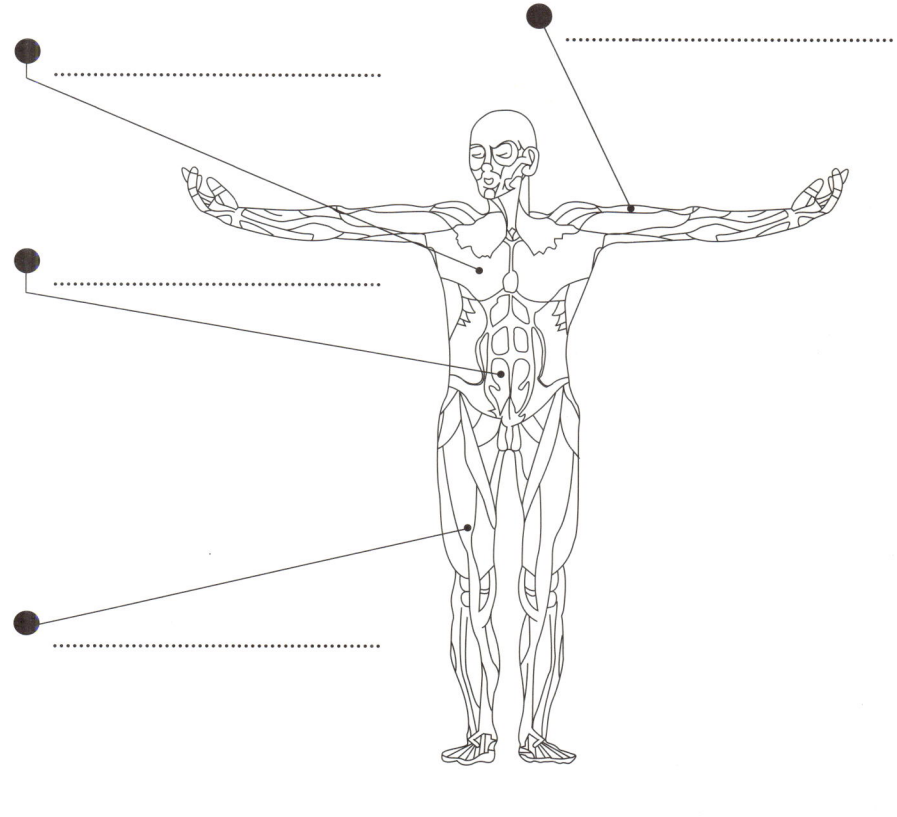

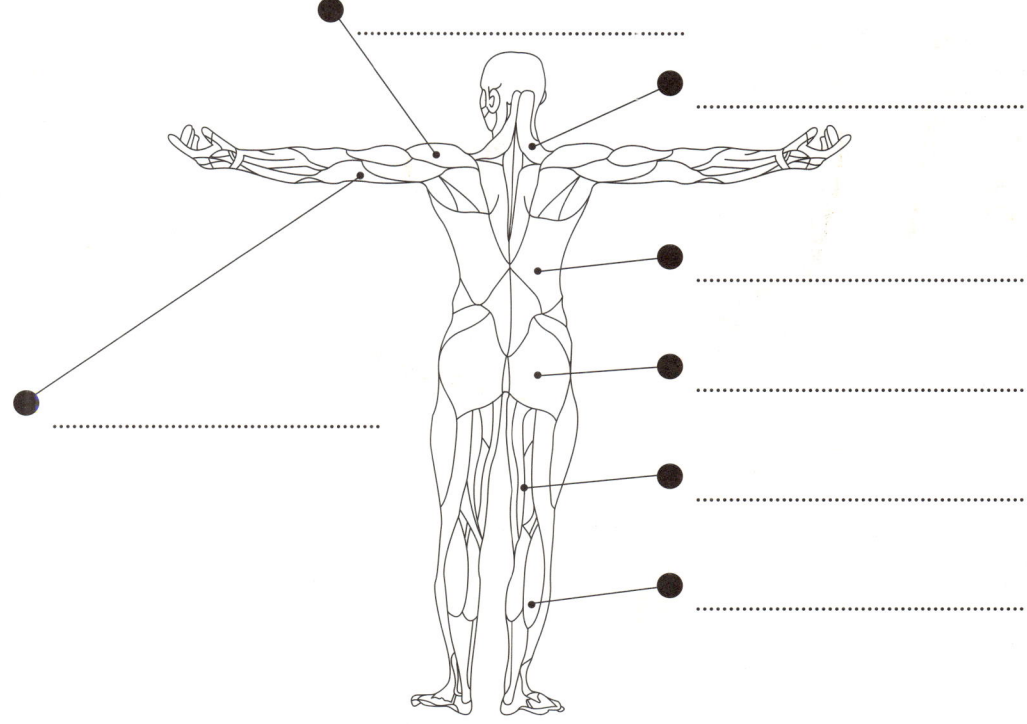

See also The World of Sport Examined Page **19**

11

The Muscular System

■ Types of muscle

1. Draw arrows to link the descriptions below with the right muscle type.
2. Complete the rest of the table.

Description	Muscle type	Where is this muscle type found?	State one other quality of this fibre
Muscle fibres never fatigue	Skeletal	....	....
Muscle fibres operate automatically	Cardiac	....	....
Muscle fibres used to perform movement in sport	Involuntary	....	....

Muscle speed

Insert the words *Fast twitch* or *Slow twitch* to complete each sentence.

a. .... fibres contract very quickly.

b. .... fibres are capable of repeated contractions over a long period of time.

c. .... fibres are capable of stronger and more powerful muscle contractions.

d. .... fibres fatigue rapidly.

e. The oxygen supply to .... fibres is very good.

f. A marathon runner will have a greater proportion of .... fibres in his/her leg muscles.

g. A sprinter will have a greater proportion of ....

.... fibres in his/her leg muscles.

See also The World of Sport Examined Pages **18-21**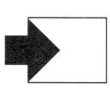

The Muscular System

■ Muscles and movement

Fill in the missing words. The first one has been done for you.
a. Isotonic contraction takes place when ...

a muscle is working concentrically or eccentrically.

....

....

b. Concentric contraction takes place when ...

....

....

c. Eccentric contraction takes place when ...

....

....

d. Isokinetic contraction occurs when ...

....

....

e. Isometric contraction takes place when ...

....

....

Muscles working together – prime movers and antagonists

Look at the diagram and fill in the missing words.
In this isotonic action the biceps muscle is the .... This muscle contracts to start
the movement. The triceps muscle is the .... This muscle ....
to allow the movement to take place.

This isotonic action is concentric. One example
of an isotonic eccentric action is

....

....

....

....

....

● ....

● ....

Tendons

Muscles are attached to bones by tendons.
The origin is at one end of the muscle. The insertion is at the other end.
How can we tell which end is which?

a. The origin is the end ....

b. The insertion is the end ....

© Andy Sibson Published by Thomas Nelson and Sons Ltd. 1997

The Muscular System

■ Posture

Muscle tone is important for good posture.
Write whether each diagram shows good posture or poor posture,
and give an explanation.

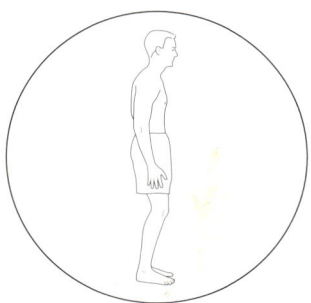

This posture is ....

because ....

....

....

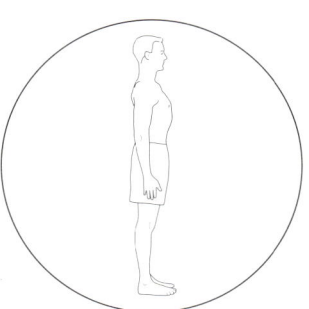

This posture is ....

because ....

....

....

This posture is ....

because ....

....

....

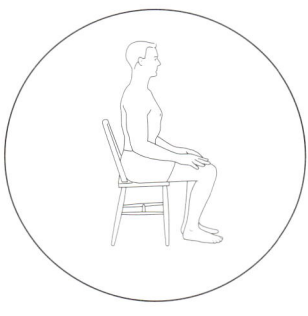

This posture is ....

because ....

....

....

This posture is ....

because ....

....

....

This posture is ....

because ....

....

....

See also The World of Sport Examined Page **23**

© Andy Sibson Published by Thomas Nelson and Sons Ltd. 1997

The Skeletal and Muscular Systems

■ Joints and muscles in action

1. Work with a partner and attempt each of the four movements listed below. Take it in turns to observe each other. Each action has two phases – preparation and the action itself.
2. Fill in the table. The first one has been done for you.

Four movements	Phases	Joint used	Type of movement	Muscle used
1. Kicking a stationary ball	Preparation			
	Lifting and drawing the leg back, to kick.	Knee	Flexion	Hamstrings
	Action			
	Kicking the ball.	Ankle	Extension	Gastrocnemius
2. Shooting for goal in netball	Preparation			
	Action			
3. Doing the pull shot in cricket	Preparation			
	Action			
4. Doing a straddle jump from the floor or trampoline	Preparation			
	Action			

© Andy Sibson Published by Thomas Nelson and Sons Ltd. 1997

See also The World of Sport Examined Pages **10-25**

Research Tasks

■ The skeletal system *See also* The World of Sport Examined Page **10**

1. Describe the process of ossification from the embryonic stage through to adulthood.
2. Describe four functions of the skeletal system and give at least two examples of each one.
3. Name the five regions of the vertebral column and explain the importance of each to body movement.
4. Define cartilage, ligaments and tendons. Explain their function within or at synovial joints.
5. Draw and describe an example of a long bone, a short bone, a flat bone and an irregular bone.
6. Name five types of movement at joints and give one example of each, other than those provided in The World of Sport Examined.

■ The muscular system *See also* The World of Sport Examined Page **18**

1. List and describe the three types of muscle found within the human body.
2. Explain how muscles work. Include the terms 'motor unit' and 'muscle fibre' in your explanation.
3. Define 'slow twitch' and 'fast twitch' muscle fibres.
4. Compare the ratio of slow to fast twitch fibres in power sportspeople and endurance athletes.
5. Describe good posture and give examples of good and bad posture when walking, sitting and lifting.
6. Muscles and leverage are linked together. Describe how bones are used as levers.
7. Give examples of second and third order levers in the body.

Revision Checklist

Tick the boxes.

■ The skeletal system

Do I ...
1. ... know how bone grows? ☐
2. ... know the four functions of the skeleton? ☐
3. ... know the names of the main bones and where they are found? ☐
4. ... understand how the vertebral column works? ☐
5. ... know where to find hinge and ball and socket joints? ☐
6. ... know what cartilage and ligaments do at a joint? ☐

Can I ...
1. ... name and describe five types of movement at joints? ☐

■ The muscular system

Do I ...
1. ... know the names of the major muscles and where they are? ☐
2. ... know where to find skeletal, smooth and cardiac muscle? ☐
3. ... understand how muscles work in pairs? ☐
4. ... know how muscles are attached to bones? ☐
5. ... know how muscles contract? ☐
6. ... know that some muscle fibres are slow twitch and some are fast twitch? ☐
7. ... know what muscle tone is? ☐
8. ... know what 'good posture' means? ☐

Can I ...
1. ... name six muscles and describe the action that they create? ☐
2. ... identify examples of isotonic and isometric muscular contraction? ☐
3. ... explain why good posture is important? ☐

© Andy Sibson Published by Thomas Nelson and Sons Ltd. 1997

See also The World of Sport Examined Pages **10-25** ➡

Revision Checklist
Tick the boxes.

■ The skeletal system

Do I ...
1. ... understand the process of bone growth? ☐
2. ... know the four functions of the skeleton? ☐
3. ... know the name and the locations of the main bones? ☐
4. ... know the function and arrangement of the five regions of the vertebral column? ☐
5. ... know the six basic types of synovial joint? ☐
6. ... understand the function of cartilage, ligaments and tendons? ☐

Can I ...
1. ... classify bones as long, short, flat and irregular? ☐
2. ... describe in detail the features of the axial and appendicular skeleton? ☐
3. ... give examples of six types of synovial joint?
4. ... accurately label a synovial joint? ☐
5. ... name and describe five types of movement at joints? ☐

■ The muscular system

Do I ...
1. ... know the name and location of each of the major muscles? ☐
2. ... know the function and location of skeletal, smooth and cardiac muscle? ☐

Can I ...
1. ... explain the key differences between fast and slow twitch muscle fibres? ☐
2. ... describe the practical application of different types of muscle fibres? ☐
3. ... explain the term 'muscle tone'? ☐
4. ... differentiate between the origin and the insertion of a muscle? ☐
5. ... name twelve muscles and describe the action that they create? ☐
6. ... identify examples of isotonic, isometric and isokinetic muscular contraction? ☐
7. ... describe good posture, and explain its importance ☐

See also The World of Sport Examined Pages **10-25** ➡

The Circulatory System

List the five functions of the circulatory system.

1. It takes ....

2. It removes ....

3. It carries ....

4. It maintains ....

5. It prevents ....

A general view of the circulatory system

1. **Label the diagram.**
2. **Colour the arteries red and the veins blue.**

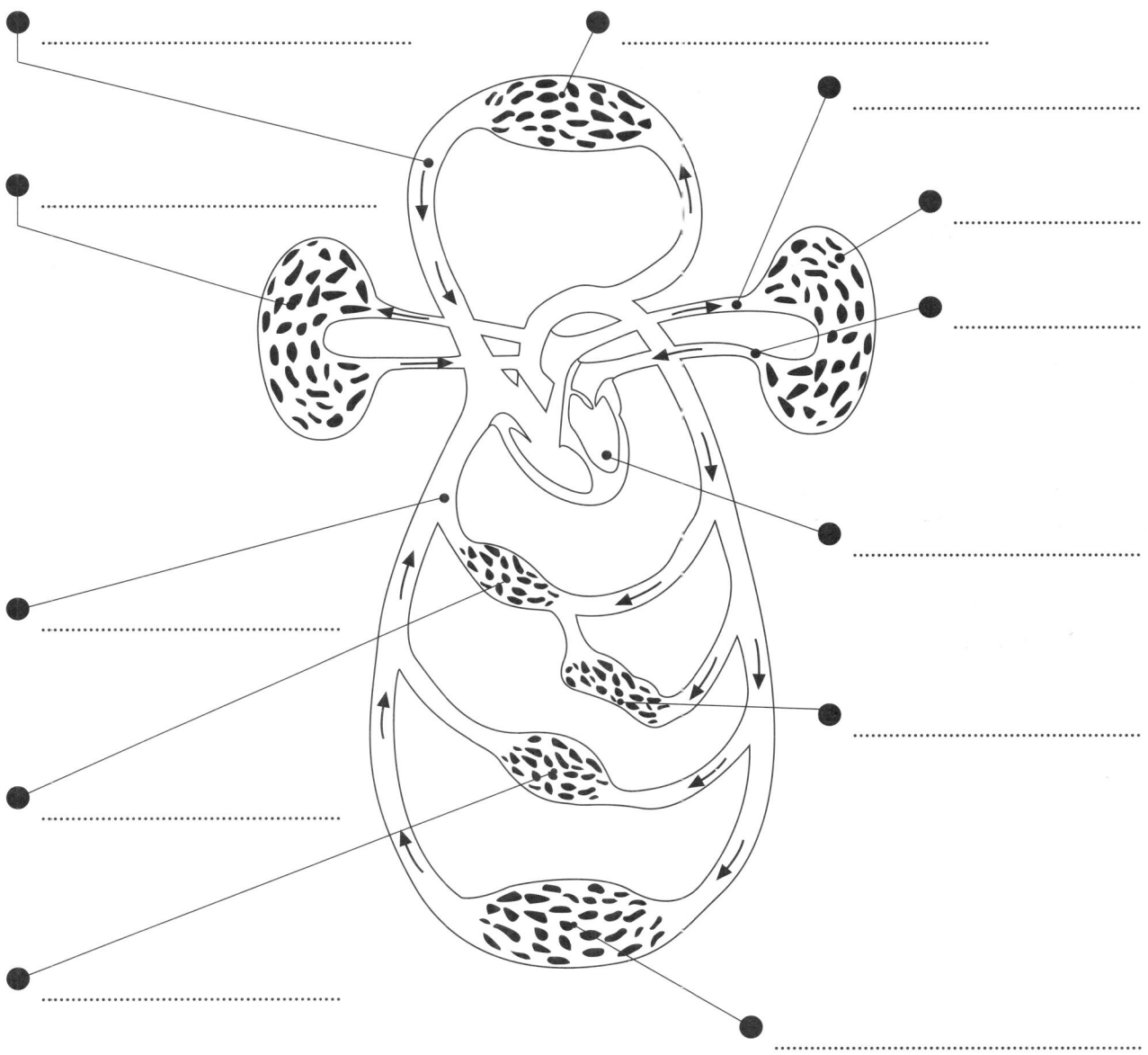

© Andy Sibson Published by Thomas Nelson and Sons Ltd. 1997

The Circulatory System

■ The heart

1. Colour arteries red and veins blue.
2. Label the diagram.

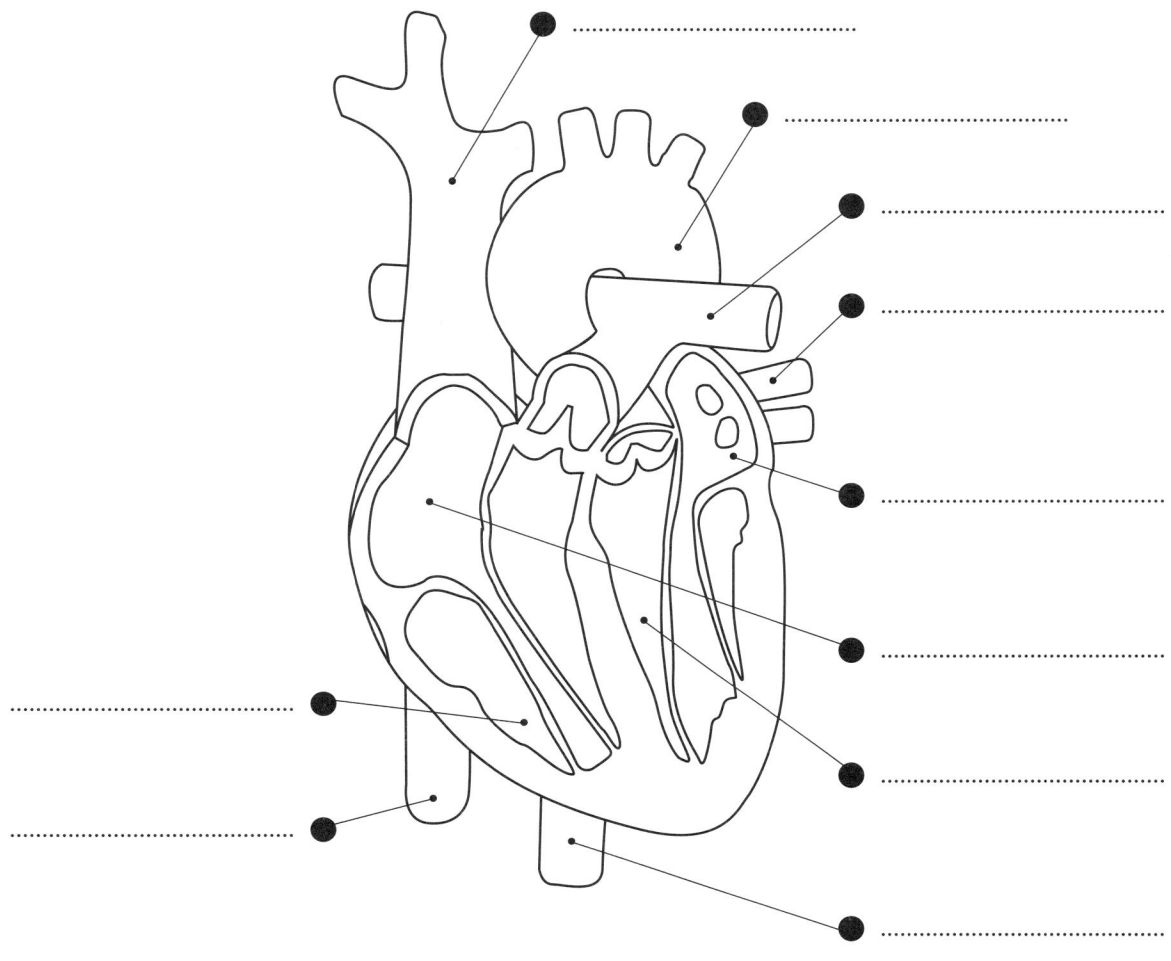

The heart is a pump that keeps blood circulating throughout the body.
The arteries carry 'red' blood out from the heart.
The veins contain 'blue' blood returning to the heart.
The artery and vein leading from the heart to the lungs are the exceptions
to the 'red'/'blue' blood rule.

3. Write the name of the artery which carries 'blue' deoxygenated blood.

....

4. Write the name of the vein which carries 'red' oxygenated blood.

....

See also The World of Sport Examined Page **27**

© Andy Sibson Published by Thomas Nelson and Sons Ltd. 1997

The Circulatory System

■ What is blood?

1. Draw arrows to link each blood component with its correct function.
2. Write down each blood component next to its function, to help you to remember it.

Blood component   **Function**

Red cells   Fight disease ➡ ....

White cells   Form blood clots ➡ ....

Plasma   Transports nutrients ➡ ....

Platelets   Carry oxygen ➡ ....

Which blood vessels are which?

Complete each sentence using the word *Arteries,*
Capillaries or Veins.

1. The walls of .... are non-elastic.

2. The walls of .... can contract to force
   blood forwards.

3. The walls of .... can expand to carry
   blood pumped by the heart.

4. Oxygen passes through the thin walls of the

   .... into the tissues.

5. Some .... have valves to keep blood
   flowing in one direction.

6. Blood travels very slowly through the narrow

   ....

7. .... carry oxygenated blood from
   the heart.

See also The World of Sport Examined Pages **28-29**

The Respiratory System

■ The lungs

1. Label the diagram.
2. Shade each part in a different colour.

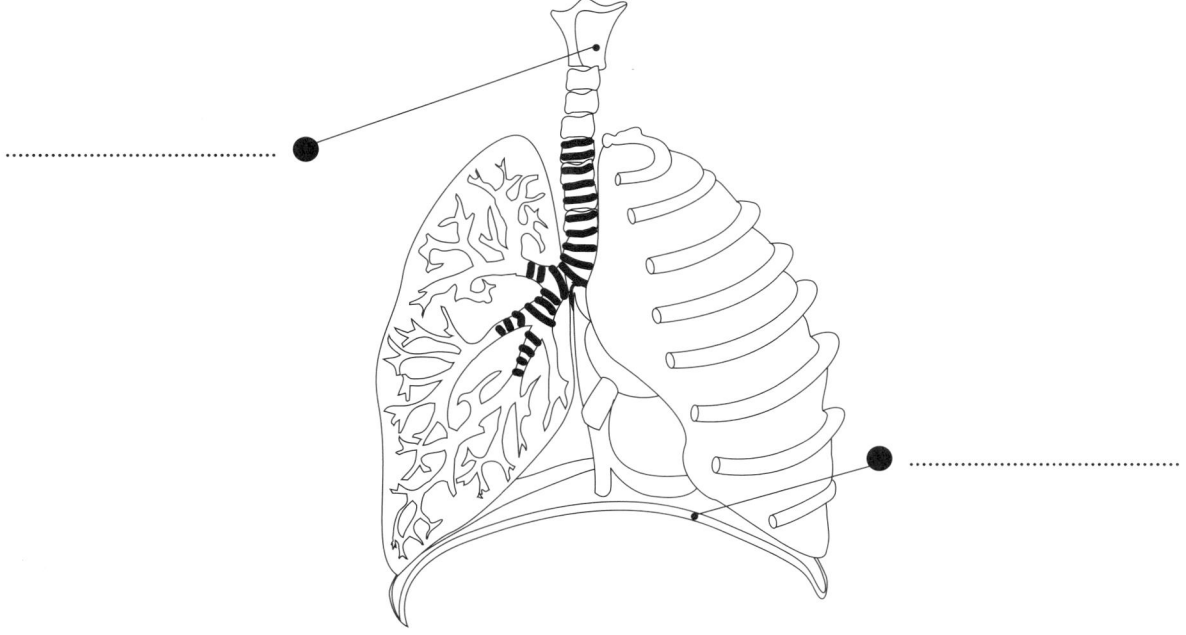

How do we breathe?

Label the diagrams below.

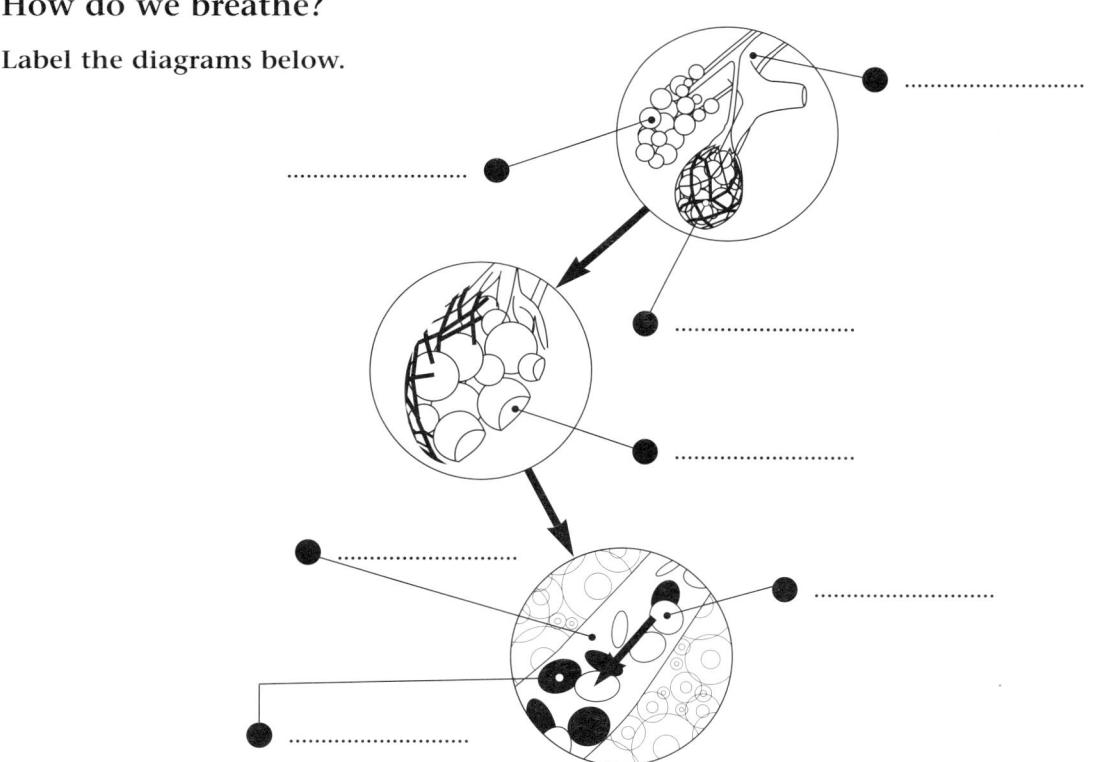

See also The World of Sport Examined Pages **32-35**

The Circulatory and Respiratory Systems

■ Checking pulse and breathing rates during exercise

1. Look at the table below.
2. Perform each activity and check your pulse and breathing rates immediately after the time period ends.
3. Complete the table.

Time period	Activity	Pulse rate (in 15 secs)	x4 per min	Breathing rate (in 15 secs)	x4 per min
–	Rest				
One minute	Walk				
Three minutes	Jog				
10-15 minutes	Play game (e.g. netball)				
20 seconds	Sprint				
Three minutes	Warm down				

Your pulse rate indicates the amount of blood flowing from your heart. The faster the rate, the more blood is being sent to the tissues. You can measure your pulse by pressing two fingers lightly on your wrist or neck and counting the number of beats.

Your breathing rate tells you how much air, and therefore oxygen, is entering your lungs and will be passed into the blood and taken to the tissues. You can measure it by placing one hand across your chest and counting the number of times that your chest rises.

4. Now plot the results on a graph to show how pulse and breathing rates are affected by exercise.

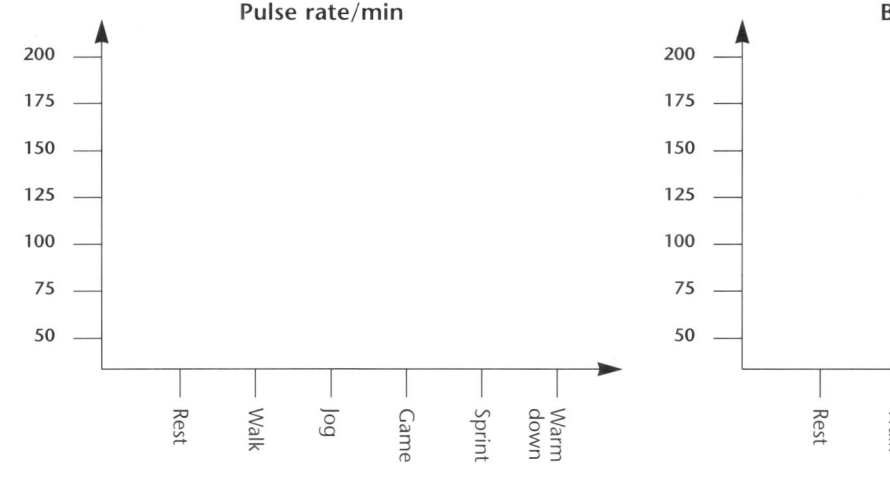

© Andy Sibson Published by Thomas Nelson and Sons Ltd. 1997

See also The World of Sport Examined Pages **26-35**

Body Systems

■ What happens when we exercise?

Use the words given to complete the sentences below.

As we exercise, our .... demand more .... The hormone .... is released. This prepares the body for the extra work-load to come. The release of hormones is controlled by the .... system. Lung capacity is increased because the abdominal muscles and .... contract more rapidly. This increases the rate at which oxygen enters the lungs and .... is removed from them. The exchange of oxygen and carbon dioxide between the alveoli and .... also improves. Cardiac output becomes greater as heart rate and .... increase dramatically. Blood flow to the .... organs is reduced to make more available for the areas in urgent need of oxygen. This is why we should not eat a lot before exercising. The whole process is planned, started and co-ordinated by the ....

Stroke volume	Nervous system	Diaphragm	Hormonal	Digestive
Muscles	Oxygen	Carbon dioxide	Adrenalin	Capillaries

■ How do we breathe?

Label the diagrams which show breathing in (inspiration) and breathing out (expiration) below.

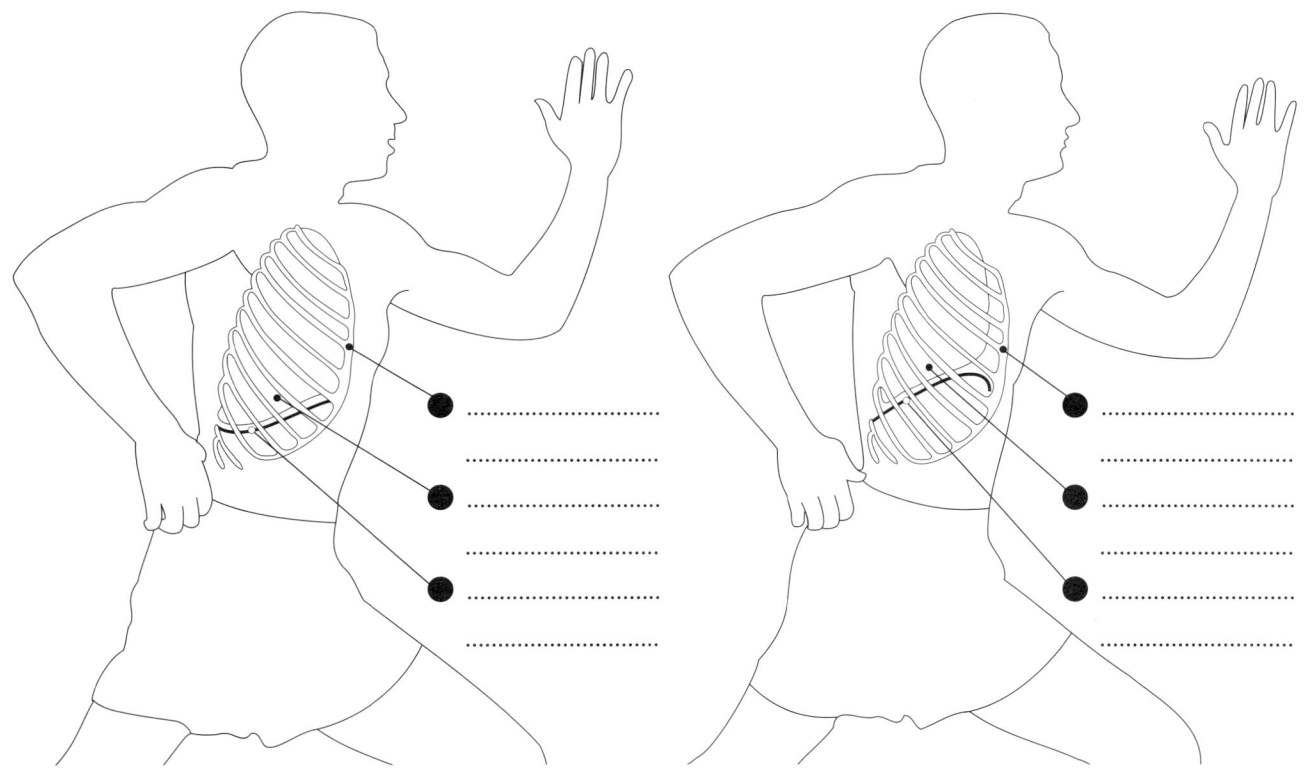

See also The World of Sport Examined Pages **32-40**

Research Tasks

■ The circulatory system *See also* The World of Sport Examined Pages **26-31**

1. Describe, in detail, the flow of blood during its journey around the body. (Use diagrams to help your explanation.)
2. Explain the changes which occur within the circulatory system during exercise.
3. Name the four main components of blood and describe the functions that each one performs.
4. Explain the process by which blood pressure is measured and recorded.

■ The respiratory system *See also* The World of Sport Examined Pages **32-35**

1. Explain the stages of inspiration and expiration of air in and out of the lungs.
2. Describe the process of gaseous exchange.
3. Explain the changes within the respiratory system during exercise.

■ Other body systems *See also* The World of Sport Examined Pages **36-40**

1. Explain how the nervous system plans, starts and co-ordinates movement.
2. List seven ways in which the hormonal system has an effect upon the body during exercise.
3. Describe how the digestive system changes food into the basic nutrients that the body needs for energy.

Revision Checklist

Tick the boxes.

■ The circulatory system

Do I ...

1. ... know how blood circulates around the body? ☐

2. ... know how 'heart rate' and 'stroke volume' produce 'cardiac output'? ☐

3. ... know the difference between arteries, veins and capillaries? ☐

4. ... know what blood pressure is? ☐

5. ... know the four things that make up blood? ☐

6. ... know what happens to our circulatory system when we exercise? ☐

Can I ...

1. ... list five functions of the circulatory system? ☐

2. ... label a diagram of the heart showing the main functions? ☐

3. ... take a pulse accurately? ☐

4. ... list three differences between an artery and a vein? ☐

5. ... explain the work of red cells, white cells, platelets and plasma? ☐

■ The respiratory system

Do I ...

1. ... understand how the diaphragm, intercostal muscles and ribs work when we breathe? ☐

2. ... know how gases are exchanged through the alveoli in the lungs and capillary walls at the working muscles? ☐

3. ... know the difference between the air breathed in and the air breathed out? ☐

Can I ...

1. ... label a diagram of the lungs and breathing system? ☐

2. ... list four things that happen to the respiratory system when we exercise? ☐

■ The nervous system

Do I ...

1. ... understand how the nervous system plans, starts and co-ordinates all human movement? ☐

■ The hormonal system

Can I ...

1. ... list five ways in which hormones affect the body during exercise? ☐

■ The digestive system

Do I ...

1. ... know how the food we eat is broken down into the basic nutrients that the body needs? ☐

See also The World of Sport Examined Pages **26-39**

Revision Checklist
Tick the boxes.

■ The circulatory system

Do I ...
1. ... understand how the circulatory system works? ☐
2. ... understand the terms 'Heart rate', 'Stroke volume' and 'Cardiac output'? ☐
3. ... know the composition of blood? ☐
4. ... know what happens to our circulatory system when we exercise? ☐

Can I ...
1. ... list five functions of the circulatory system? ☐
2. ... identify the main elements of the heart and circulatory system? ☐
3. ... take a pulse accurately? ☐
4. ... explain what blood pressure is and how it is recorded? ☐
5. ... list three differences between an artery and a vein? ☐
6. ... explain the roles of red cells, white cells, platelets and plasma? ☐

■ The respiratory system

Do I ...
1. ... understand the action of the diaphragm, intercostal muscles and ribs when breathing? ☐
2. ... know how to test lung capacity? ☐

Can I ...
1. ... identify the main elements of the lungs and respiratory system? ☐
2. ... explain the process of gaseous exchange? ☐
3. ... explain what happens to the respiratory system when we exercise? ☐

■ The nervous system

Can I ...
1. ... explain how the nervous system plans, starts and co-ordinates all human movement? ☐

■ The hormonal system

Can I ...
1. ... list and explain eight ways in which hormones affect the body during exercise? ☐

■ The digestive system

Do I ...
1. ... know how the digestive system changes food into basic nutrients? ☐

© Andy Sibson Published by Thomas Nelson and Sons Ltd. 1997

See also The World of Sport Examined Pages **26-39** ➡

How does our Body get Energy?

Fill in the missing words.

Our bodies get energy from .... ,

.... and .... in our food. They can

only use energy when it is in the form of a chemical compound called

.... Only a small amount of ....

can be stored in the body (enough for five – eight seconds of hard

work). So, our body has to keep .... it.

■ The three energy systems

There are three energy systems which work together to make sure that our muscles are getting energy in the form of ATP.

1. Creatine phosphate system

This is a high ....

.... which is stored in our muscles. Breaking it down will give enough

energy for ....
of hard work.

Energy from the creatine phosphate system is available

instantly, but ....

....

....

....

....

2. Lactic acid system

This system supplies energy until we can get enough

....

to our muscles. It uses

.... which is

stored in the ....

and ....

It produces energy, but

also ....

.... which

causes pain in the muscles.

The lactic acid system is very

important when ....

....

....

....

....

3. Aerobic system

The energy that this system provides is almost

....

When our muscles have

enough ....
they get energy from breaking

down ....

and ....

We use the aerobic system in

most of our ....
It provides energy too slowly

for ....
activities, but it is important
for sportspeople who need to

....

....

....

....

Oxygen debt

After exercising using these systems we continue to breathe heavily. We have been using more oxygen than we have. Paying back our oxygen debt allows us to:

1. ....

2. ....

3. ....

See also The World of Sport Examined Pages **42-46**

Energy from ATP

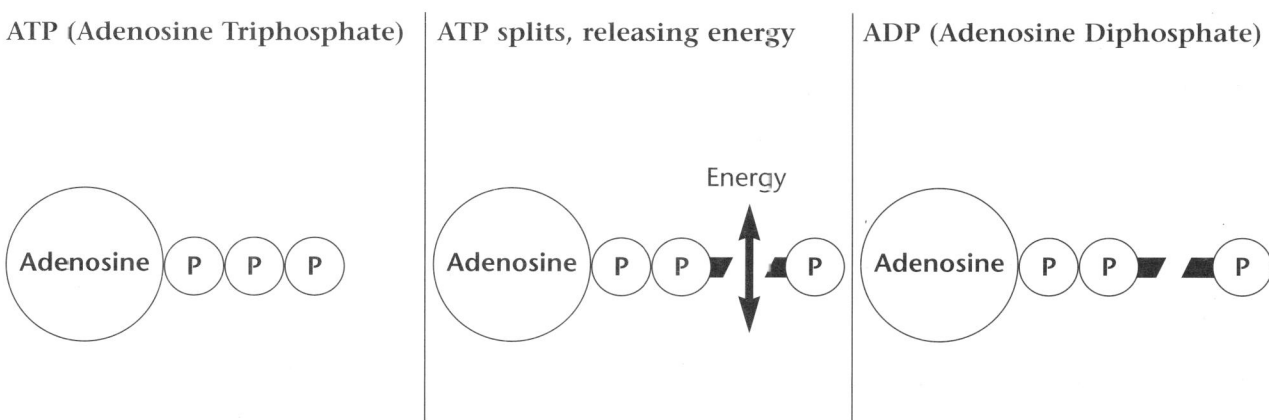

ATP (Adenosine Triphosphate)	ATP splits, releasing energy	ADP (Adenosine Diphosphate)

ATP can be reformed (or, replenished) in three ways: through the creatine phosphate system; the lactic acid system; or, the aerobic system. Complete the chart below to show the activities which typically use each system.

Short term energy system creating oxygen debt		Long term energy system – no oxygen debt
Creatine phosphate system	**Lactic acid system**	**Aerobic system**
Lasts for up to 20 seconds Typical activities using this system:	(Anaerobic glycolysis) Lasts for 30 seconds to two minutes. Typical activities using this system:	(Aerobic metabolism) Lasts almost indefinitely. Typical activities using this system: ....

See also The World of Sport Examined Page **42-48**

Training Zones

■ Maximum heart rate

By calculating our maximum heart rate (MHR) we can work out our
own thresholds for both aerobic and anaerobic training.
MHR = 220 – your age.
Fill in the missing words.
To calculate our MHR: 220 – .... (your age) = ... beats per minute.

To train our aerobic system we should work at .... % of MHR.

To train our anaerobic system we should work at .... % of MHR.

The required heart rates for various training effects for a 16 year old

Label the diagram to show the training zones for each type of fitness.

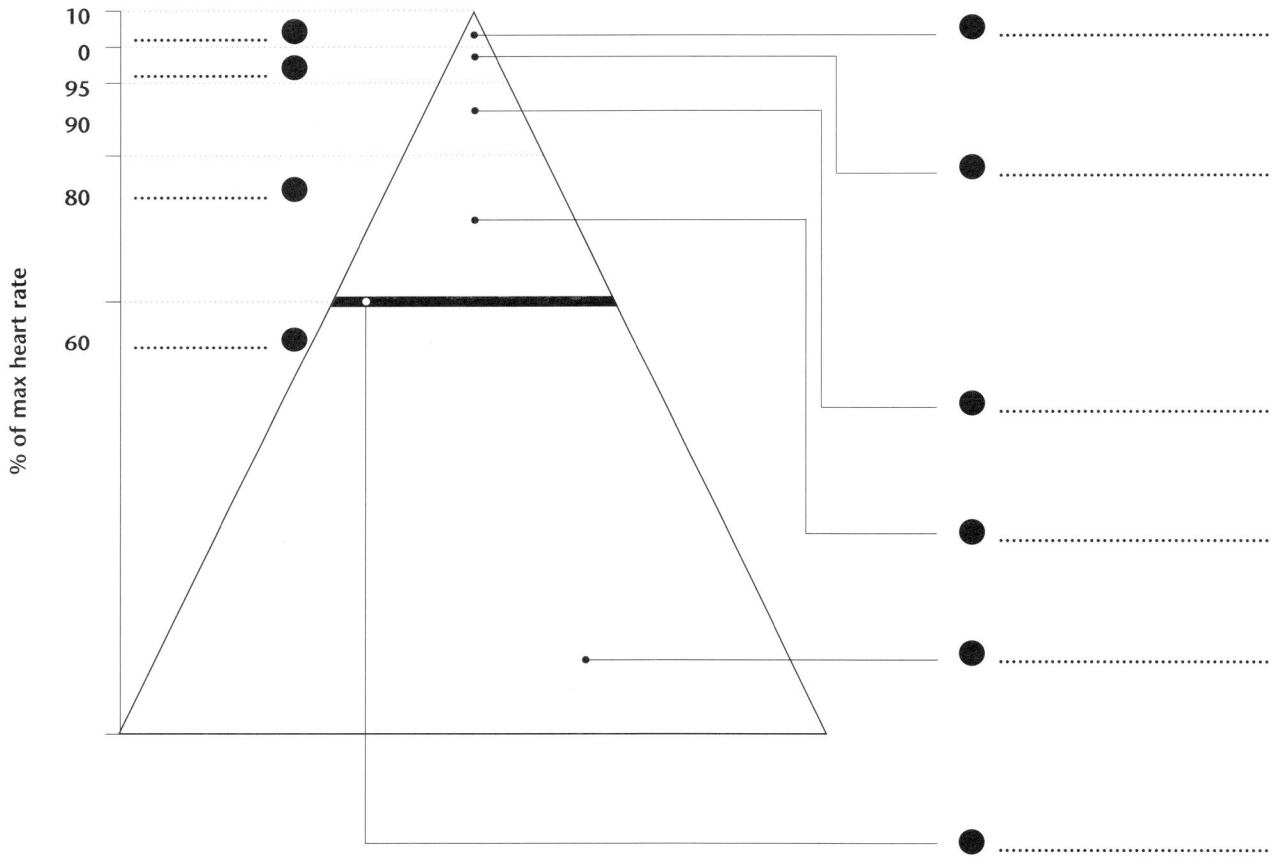

See also The World of Sport Examined Page **48**

© Andy Sibson Published by Thomas Nelson and Sons Ltd. 1997

Improving Performance

Sportsmen and sportswomen are constantly searching for ways to improve their individual and team performances.
There are three areas in which improvement can take place:
1. Fitness;
2. Skill;
3. Strategies and tactics.

Fitness

Everyone needs to be healthy. Health related fitness improves the quality of our lives. Sport related fitness goes beyond the day-to-day requirements of most people.
Coaches and performers must understand how the body works in order to know the likely effects of training exercises. They must also understand the demands of the sport for which they are training.
There are many training methods, but exercises selected must be specific to the sport so that the right kind of fitness is developed.

Skill

The development of skill requires the efforts of the performers and their teachers and coaches over a long period of time.
The performer must remain motivated and must be constantly informed of the progress that is being made. Being in the right frame of mind is essential for skill development and performance.
The coach plays a crucial role in this psychological aspect of sport.

Strategies and tactics

As the level of competition increases, teams and individual performers become involved in battles to outwit each other. Often a player or team with a better strategy will beat more skilful opponents. When players and teams are already highly skilful, training time can be devoted to preparing strategies. However, within competition, players need to respond to changing circumstances. So, as well as having prepared strategies, they need to be able to adapt to each situation.

See also The World of Sport Examined Pages **50-102**

Body Types

There are three main body types: endomorph, mesomorph and ectomorph.
We are all part endomorph, part mesomorph and part ectomorph.
Our body type, along with our body size (height compared to
weight) and body composition (amount of fat), indicates the kind
of sports at which we might be successful.

1. Label the diagrams of extreme body types.
2. Add a description of each below.
3. List sports for which each type is well suited.

This body type is a:	This body type is a:	This body type is a:
....	....	....
These have	These have	These have ....
....	....	....
....	....	....
....	....	....
....	....	....
....	....	....
Suitable sports:	Suitable sports:	Suitable sports:
....	....	....
....	....	....
....	....	....
....	....	....
....	....	....

See also The World of Sport Examined Page **59**

Health Related Fitness Testing

1. Select a fitness test from 'The World of Sport Examined'
   for each type of fitness.
2. Complete the test and record your score on the table.
3. Train and retest after six weeks.
4. Record your new score.

Type of fitness	Name and description of test	My score	
		Test	Retest
VO₂ max (stamina)			
Maximum (static) strength			
Muscular power*			
Muscular endurance*			
Flexibility			

* Muscular power and muscular endurance can also be classified as sport related fitnesses.

See also The World of Sport Examined Pages **54-63**

Sport Related Fitness Testing

1. Select a fitness test from 'The World of Sport Examined' for each type of fitness.
2. Complete the test and record your score on the table.
3. Train and retest after six weeks.
4. Record your new score.

Type of fitness	Name and description of test	My score	
		Test	Retest
Reaction time*			
Speed			
Co-ordination			
Agility			
Balance			

* Simple reaction time cannot be improved through training.

See also The World of Sport Examined Pages **64-68**

© Andy Sibson Published by Thomas Nelson and Sons Ltd. 1997

Fitness Match

1. Select your best sport and look at its fitness requirements.
2. Mark them on the chart.
3. Look at your levels of fitness by doing the tests on the chart below.
4. Grade yourself using the tables in 'The World of Sport Examined'.
5. Mark your fitness levels, in a different colour, on the chart.
6. Look at the chart to see the areas in which you need to train harder to improve your performance.

Name: .... Sport: ....

Personal fitness level

Test	High	Above average	Average	Below average	Low	Fitness requirements of the sport
Stork stand						Balance
Alternate hand wall toss						Co-ordination
Sit and reach						Flexibility
Illinois agility run						Agility
NCF abdominal curl						Muscular endurance
Hand grip dynamometer						Maximum strength
Standing broad jump						Muscular power
Cooper 12 minute run						Stamina

See also The World of Sport Examined Pages **54-68**    35

Age and Sport

■ You are never too old ...

Exercise is vital for health and growth during childhood. We reach our physical prime in our late twenties and early thirties. After this age, our physical powers decline by about one to two percent a year.

These athletes are still running, but will face some problems due to the ageing process.

Complete the sentences below.

As we get older, our maximum heart rate ....

Our arteries .... , increasing ....

and reducing ....

Our VO$_2$ max .... Our maximum strength ....,

due to .... Our muscles change ....

We increase our .... This is due to ....

However, if we continue to exercise regularly we can ....

....

See also The World of Sport Examined Page **83**

Gender and Sport

■ Sports spot the difference

One of the major things which decides our sporting potential is our gender (whether we are male or female). Boys and girls mature at about the same rate until the age of nine or ten, but then body changes mean that sporting competition between the sexes is not always fair. There are physical differences between men and women that must be considered. However, the differences in times and distances achieved in sport between men and women are becoming smaller.

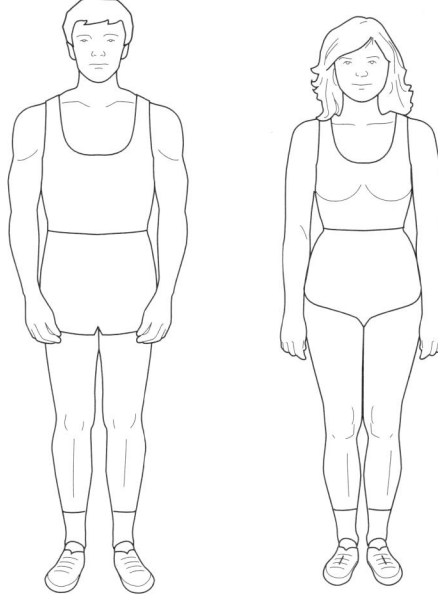

Complete the table below to show the differences in body size, strength and aerobic power between the man and woman athlete.

	Men	Women
Body size		
Strength		
Aerobic power		

See also The World of Sport Examined Page **84**

Training Programmes

■ The principles of training

We should apply the SPORT principles to all training programmes.
Write what each letter stands for below.

S .... – match the training to the sport or event;

P .... – gradually increase the work load;

O .... – make the body systems work harder than normal;

R .... – we lose fitness if we do not keep training;

T .... – use a variety of methods to prevent boredom.

■ Designing a one year training programme

We must always plan ahead so that we peak, or perform at our best, at the times of major competitions. A one year training programme can be planned across four periods.

1. **Complete the table below. Name the four training seasons in the top boxes.**
2. **Describe the emphasis for each season below.**

1.	2.	3.	4. ....
....	....	....	....
....	....	....	....
....	....	....	....
....	....	....	....
....	....	....	....

■ Individual training sessions

An individual training session should consist of four phases. List these below.

1. .... 2. ....

3. .... 4. ....

■ The FITT principles

We can use the FITT principles when planning fitness programmes.
Write what each letter stands for below.

F .... – train at least three times a week. Space out sessions to recover;

I .... – work hard enough to make the body systems adapt;

T .... – each session must last at least 20 minutes at 70-75% MHR;

T .... – we must match training activities to the needs of our sport.

See also The World of Sport Examined Pages **72-75**

© Andy Sibson Published by Thomas Nelson and Sons Ltd. 1997

A. Training Methods

Below are descriptions of three different training methods.
Write the name of each.
Give examples of sports, or athletic events, for which each is suitable.

1. ....

This training method involves exercise
without rest intervals. There are two types:
Long/slow distance involves whole body
activity between 60-80% MHR and is good
for general conditioning work.
High intensity work at 85-95% MHR improves
speed and endurance.

Suitable for:

Long/slow distance

....

....

High intensity

....

....

....

2. ....

'Speed play' is the English term for this
training method. It involves varying the pace
at which we walk, run or cycle and the type of
terrain we travel over. It is good for improving
VO$_2$ max and our recovery process.

Suitable for:

....

....

....

....

3. ....

This training method involves alternating
periods of work with periods of rest. Training
sessions can be longer because the rest periods
allow us to recover. We can vary:
- the time or distance of each period
  of work;
- the amount of effort (intensity);
- the length of time we rest for;
- the type of activity we do when resting;
- the number of work and recovery periods
  in each session.

Suitable for:

....

....

....

See also The World of Sport Examined Pages **76-77**

B. Training Methods

Below are descriptions of three different training methods.
Write the name of each.
Give examples of sports, or athletic events, for which each
is suitable.

1. ....

This training method is the most popular form of resistance training. It can be designed for our particular sport. The SPORT principle should be followed when using this method. With this method we perform reps and sets. Reps are the number of times we repeat an exercise without resting.
Sets are the number of reps done in succession, e.g. one set equals ten reps.

Suitable for:

....

....

....

2. ....

These methods involve stretching a muscle before it contracts. In these exercises we use bounds, hops, jumps, leaps, skips, ricochets, swings and twists.
We should do this on grass, or on mats in the gym, to avoid joint injury.

Suitable for:

....

....

....

3. ....

We perform a series of selected exercises, or activities, in a given sequence. These can be designed to improve aerobic or anaerobic fitness. We can make the exercises more difficult by:
• increasing the number of stations;
• increasing the time spent at each station;
• increasing the number of reps at each station;
• increasing the number of complete sets of exercises we complete.

Suitable for:

....

....

....

See also The World of Sport Examined Pages **76-77**

© Andy Sibson Published by Thomas Nelson and Sons Ltd. 1997

Planning a Training Session

Prepare a training session specific to your chosen sport. Be sure to consider periodisation. You must match what you include in the training session with the phase, or training season, of the year in which it is to fit.

Name of sport: .... Training phase: ....

Warm down	Skill development phase	Fitness phase	Warm up

See also The World of Sport Examined Pages **70-84**

An Annual Training Schedule

1. Prepare a specific training schedule. List the key aspects of each training session in each of the periods.
2. Enter the months which fall into each period for your chosen sport.

Name of sport: ....

Months	Warm up	Fitness phase	Skill development phase	Warm down

See also The World of Sport Examined Pages **70-84**

Research Tasks

■ Energy in action *See also* The World of Sport Examined Pages **42-49**

1. List the reasons why our bodies need energy.
2. Describe the three energy systems within our bodies. Explain how they work and when they are used.
3. Explain how knowledge of energy systems helps us to focus our training precisely. Include the term VO_2 max in your explanation.

■ Fitness for health and performance *See also* The World of Sport Examined Pages **52-53**

Explain the meanings of the terms 'Health' and 'Fitness'.
Discuss the similarities and differences between the two.

■ Training for success *See also* The World of Sport Examined Pages **70-82**

1. List and describe each of the five principles of training.
2. Describe the FITT principle.
3. List and explain the four phases of an individual training session.
4. Produce a table or diagram to illustrate the long term effects of aerobic training.
5. List the long term effects of anaerobic training.
6. List the long term effects of resistance training and explain how different types of training improve different types of strength.

Revision Checklist
Tick the boxes.

■ Energy in action

Do I ...

1. ... know what oxygen debt is and when it occurs? ☐

Can I ...

1. ... name the three energy systems? ☐

2. ... explain the difference between the lactic acid (anaerobic) and the aerobic energy system? ☐

■ Fitness for health and performance

Do I ...

1. ... know the difference between health and fitness? ☐

2. ... know the three body types? ☐

3. ... know what muscular strength is? ☐

4. ... know what muscular endurance is? ☐

5. ... know what flexibility is? ☐

Can I ...

1. ... match a sport to each of the three body types? ☐

2. ... name a test for each of the following types of health related fitness: cardio-vascular, muscular strength, muscular endurance, flexibility? ☐

3. ... name a test for each of the following types of sport related fitness: agility, reaction time, speed, balance, co-ordination? ☐

■ Training for success

Do I ...

1. ... know the five principles of training? ☐

2. ... know which type of training improves strength? ☐

3. ... know which type of training improves endurance? ☐

4. ... know which type of training improves flexibility? ☐

5. ... know what the FITT principle is? ☐

6. ... know what is meant by cardio-vascular fitness? ☐

7. ... know that we need to match training to age, sex and other individual differences? ☐

Can I ...

1. ... list four different training methods? ☐

2. ... plan an annual training programme for my chosen sport? ☐

3. ... plan a detailed training session for my chosen sport? ☐

4. ... calculate the training threshold (heart rate target zone)? ☐

See also The World of Sport Examined Pages **42-84**

© Andy Sibson Published by Thomas Nelson and Sons Ltd. 1997

Revision Checklist
Tick the boxes.

■ Energy in action

Do I ...

1. ... understand the term 'oxygen debt' and how this occurs? ☐

Can I ...

1. ... explain how ATP is reformed through:

the creatine phosphate system;

the lactic acid (anaerobic system);

the aerobic system? ☐

■ Fitness for health and performance

Do I ...

1. ... know the three body types? ☐

Can I ...

1. ... explain the difference between health and fitness? ☐

2. ... define muscular strength, muscular endurance and flexibility? ☐

3. ... match sports to the requirement for each of the above? ☐

4. ... match the three body types to specific sports? ☐

5. ... name and explain a test for each of the following types of health related fitness: stamina, muscular strength, muscular power, muscular endurance, flexibility? ☐

6. ... name and explain a test for each of the following types of sport related fitness: speed, reaction time, co-ordination, agility, balance? ☐

■ Training for success

Do I ...

1. ... know the five principles of training? ☐

2. ... know which type of training improves strength? ☐

3. ... know which type of training improves endurance? ☐

4. ... know which type of training improves flexibility? ☐

5. ... know what the FITT principle is? ☐

6. ... know what is meant by cardio-vascular fitness? ☐

7. ... understand the need to match training to age, sex and other individual differences? ☐

Can I ...

1. ... list and explain six specific training methods? ☐

2. ... plan an annual training programme for two different sports? ☐

3. ... plan a detailed training session for two different sports? ☐

4. ... calculate the training threshold (heart rate target zone)? ☐

© Andy Sibson Published by Thomas Nelson and Sons Ltd. 1997

See also The World of Sport Examined Pages **42-84** ➡

What is Skill?

We often use the terms 'Ability', 'Technique' and 'Skill' when talking
about players. Complete the following sentences.

Ability is ....

Techniques are ....

We can combine a number of different techniques into a pattern of movement.
This is what we call skill. Complete the following sentence.

Skill is ....

We are not born with skill. We have to learn how to be skilful.

Write what the letters below stand for.

A .... + L .... + P .... = S .... (ALPS)

■ Open and closed skills

There is a difference between skills that are open and skills that are closed.
Complete the following sentences.

Open skills are ....

Closed skills are ....

Some games have a mixture of open and closed skills within them.
We can place them on a skills continuum. Look at the examples in
'The World of Sport Examined' and then place the following
activities on the skills continuum below.

Football	Darts	Boxing	Rowing	Netball	Shot putt

 Open • Closed

See also The World of Sport Examined Pages **88-89**

Motivation and Personality

■ Motivation

Motivation is a psychological factor that affects performance.
Fill in the missing words below.

When we play for fun our motivation is ....

It comes from our own inner drives.

When we play for rewards, or to please other people, our motivation

is .... If we become bored or tired, we lose

motivation and our performance gets worse.

Arousal

'Psyching up' for sport is common and it helps performance. But if our

arousal level is too high we may become too ....

and our performance may become less ....

■ Personality

Our personality is linked to our success or failure in different sports.
Fill in the missing words below.

.... are very confident and socially outgoing.

.... are less confident and socially quiet and shy.

Research suggests that extroverts and introverts prefer different types of sport.
Give examples below.

Extroverts   Introverts

....

....

....

....

....

....

However, successful sportspeople have a wide variety of different personalities.
It is important to treat all sportspeople as individuals.

See also The World of Sport Examined Pages **92-94**

How do we Learn Skills?

■ Feedback

Feedback gives us vital information about our performances.
It enables us to analyse and improve them.
Below are four descriptions of different types of feedback.
Write the name of each type against the description that fits.

1. .... This feedback comes to us from our own senses. We know how the shot felt and our eyes tell us whether or not we were successful.

2. .... We receive this feedback by listening to our coach, being given our score or seeing ourselves on video.

3. .... This feedback tells us how well we have done. Did we score a goal? How many points did we get? What position did we finish in the race?

4. .... This feedback is to do with how well we performed rather than the actual result of our performance. We know when we have done our best.

■ Guidance

Guidance is given in three ways: visual, verbal and manual. Give examples below.

1. Visual: ....

2. Verbal: ....

3. Manual: ....

■ Practise

By practising skills regularly, we reach the stage where we can perform them automatically. Then we can concentrate on tactics and strategies.

See also The World of Sport Examined Pages **91 and 97**

The Information Processing Model

The Information Processing Model (IPM) is a theory about how we perform skills. There are four processes in this model: input, decision-making, output and feedback. Explain each of these on the chart below.

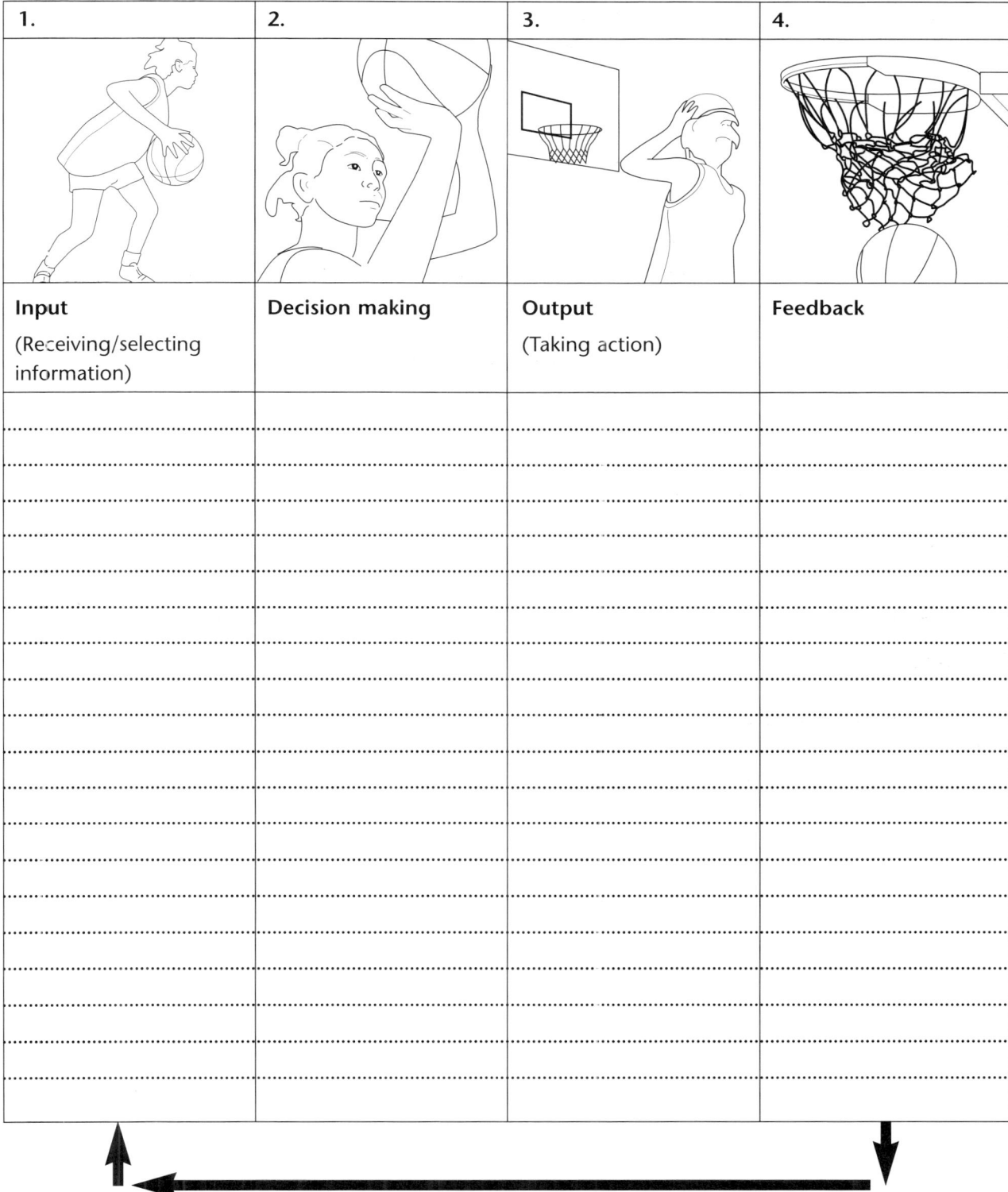

1.	2.	3.	4.
Input (Receiving/selecting information)	**Decision making**	**Output** (Taking action)	**Feedback**

See also The World of Sport Examined Pages **90-91**   49

Setting Goals for Success

There are two types of sporting goals, these are outcome goals and performance goals. Give an example of each below.

Outcome goals: ....

Performance goals: ....

We set performance goals in order to achieve success. Success increases confidence and motivation. The National Coaching Foundation (N.C.F.) has found a way to write performance goals. Write down what SMARTER stands for, and give the meaning of each word.

S .... ➡ ....

M................................. ➡ ....

A .... ➡ ....

R .... ➡ ....

T .... ➡ ....

E .... ➡ ....

R .... ➡ ....

Set a SMARTER performance goal for yourself, from your own sport. See 'The World of Sport Examined' for an example from volleyball to help you.

S .... ➡ ....

M................................. ➡ ....

A .... ➡ ....

R .... ➡ ....

T .... ➡ ....

E .... ➡ ....

R .... ➡ ....

Tick and date this box when you have achieved your goal.

Tick	Date

© Andy Sibson Published by Thomas Nelson and Sons Ltd. 1997

See also The World of Sport Examined Page **93**

A Balanced Diet

1. **Fill in the missing words below.**
   We need food for .... , ... , ...

   and ....
**A balanced diet ensures that we get enough of all of the types
of food that we need.**
2. **Complete the diagram to show what makes up a balanced diet.**

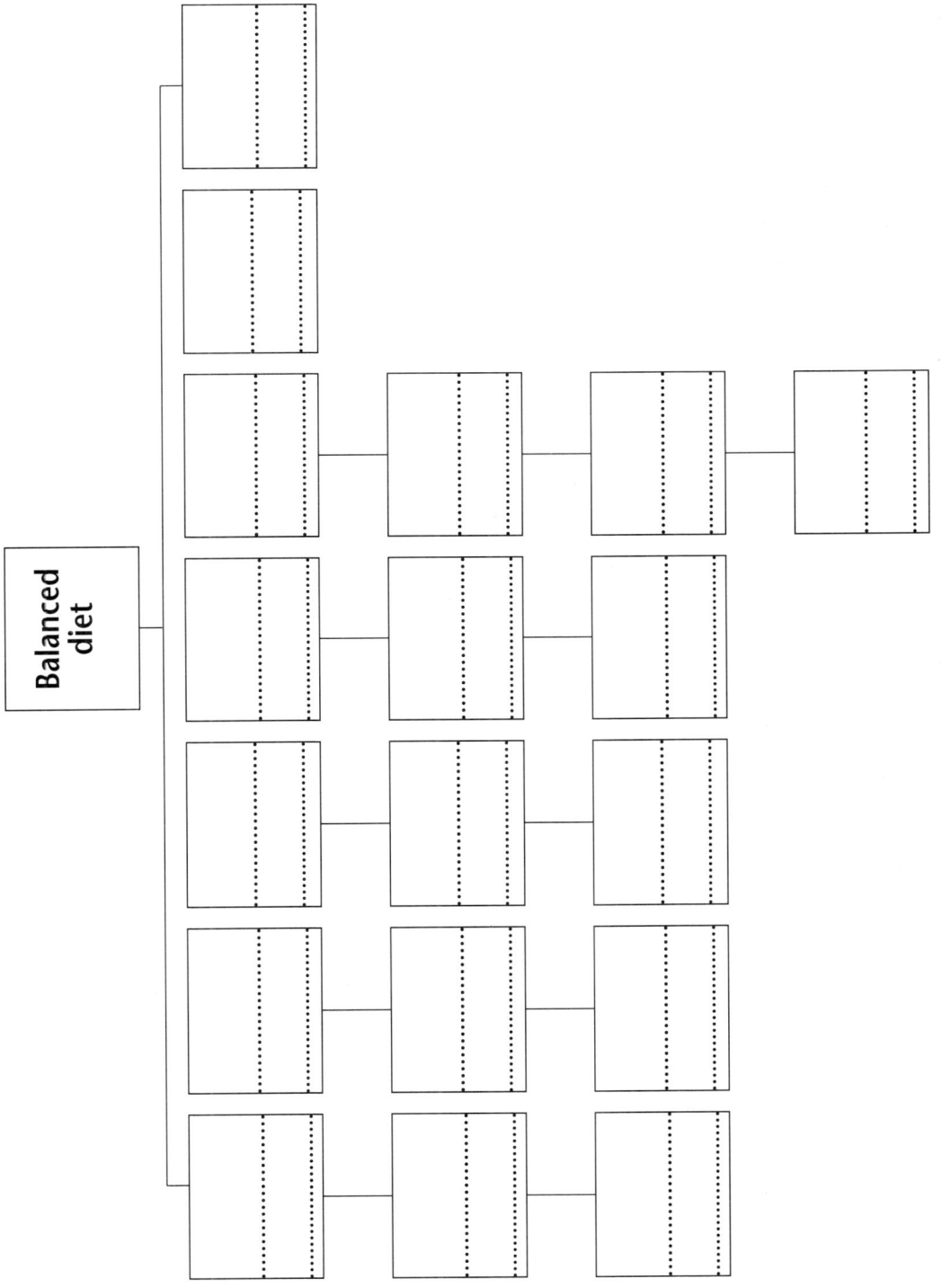

The Seven Essential Components

Complete the chart below.

Food type		Why is this important?	What foods do we find this in?
1. Carbohydrates:	Sugar		
	Starch		
2. Fats:	Saturated		
	Unsaturated		
3. Proteins:			
4. Vitamins:	A		
	C		
	D		
5. Minerals:	Calcium		
	Iron		
	Iodine		
6. Fibre			
7. Water			

See also The World of Sport Examined Pages **106-109**

The Energy Equation

Our diet, weight and energy needs are linked together. Many types
of diet and diet schemes attempt to complicate the simple facts
about weight gain and weight loss.

1. Label each of the diagrams below.
2. Write a sentence to explain each diagram.

See also The World of Sport Examined Pages **111-112**

Dietary Advice

Interview one of your parents or grandparents.
1. List the food and drink that they have consumed in one typical day.
2. Write down the amount of activity they have had during that day.

Food and drink	Activity

3. Write a summary about the effects that their diet and
   activity pattern will have on their weight.

....

....

....

4. Write down the advice you would offer them about this.

....

....

....

....

....

See also The World of Sport Examined Pages **106-113** ➡

Hygiene

1. Write down what hygiene means.

....

....

....

....

2. Make brief notes about each feature listed below.

Skin	....
Acne	....
Clothing	....
Nails	....
Jewellery	....
Hair	....
Teeth	....
Feet	....
Athlete's foot	....
Verrucas	....

How we Affect our Performance

■ Sleep and rest

**Read 'The World of Sport Examined' page 115 and complete
the sentences below.**

Sleep

Most people need between .... and .... hours sleep per night.

If our sleep is disturbed then our sporting performance ....

Our sleep can be disturbed by .... , ... ,

or ...., eating .... meals

or ....

Rest

Rest is vital for our body to .... from the activities of the day.

It is especially important for ....

■ Cigarettes and alcohol

Read pages 116-7 and list the effects of drinking and smoking on performance.

Drinking alcohol

1. ....
2. ....
3. ....
4. ....
5. ....
6. ....

Smoking cigarettes

1. ....
2. ....
3. ....
4. ....
5. ....
6. ....

■ Drugs

Read page 118 and fill in the missing words below.

Drugs are defined as .... Some can be used to improve sports performance.

The use of banned drugs in sport is called ....

Give three reasons why doping is not allowed.

1. ....
2. ....
3. ....

Give the four main reasons why sportspeople take drugs to improve performance.

1. .... 2 ....

3. .... 4. ....

See also The World of Sport Examined Pages **114-123**

Drugs to Aid Performance

The classes of drugs shown on the diagram below are
banned in many sports. Write a brief description of the effect
each type of drug would have on an athlete.

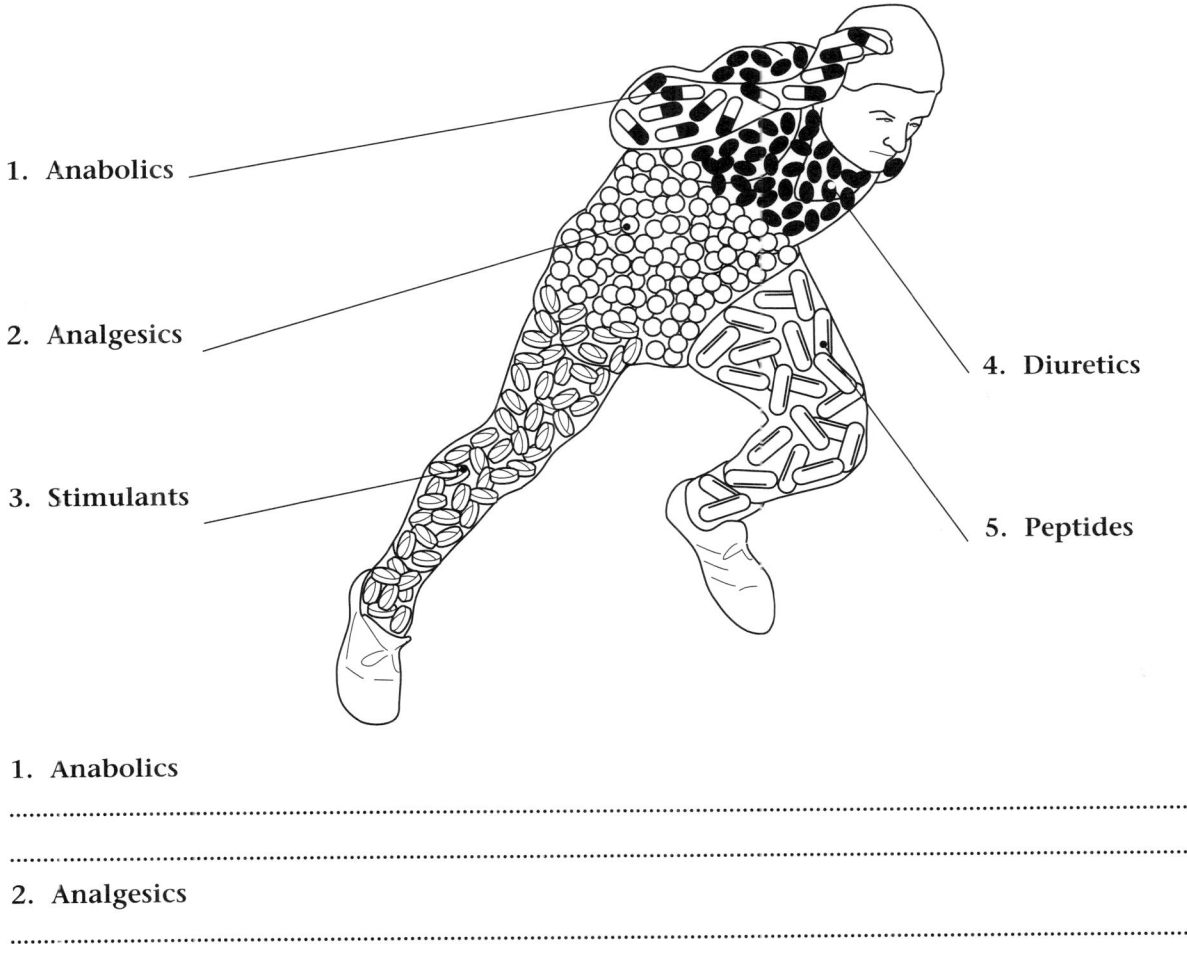

1. Anabolics

2. Analgesics

3. Stimulants

4. Diuretics

5. Peptides

1. **Anabolics**

....

....

2. **Analgesics**

....

....

3. **Stimulants**

....

....

4. **Diuretics**

....

....

5. **Peptides**

....

....

See also The World of Sport Examined Pages **119-121**

Drug Testing

Drugs which improve sports performance are banned because they are harmful to health, damage the image of sport and are a way of cheating. The International Olympic Committee (I.O.C.) has an international drug code and all sports federations must follow it. In Britain, the Sports Council tests sportspeople in and out of competition.

■ How is drug testing organised?

Fill in the spaces below to show each stage of the drug testing process during competition.

1. ....

   .... ⬇

2. ....

   .... ⬇

3. ....

   .... ⬇

4. ....

   .... ⬇

5. ....

   .... ⬇

6. .... ➡ .... ➡ ....

   .... ⬇

7. ....

   .... ⬇

8. ....

   .... ⬇

9. ....

   ....

In some sports, random out-of-season tests have caught a number of drug takers. However, the drug testers are always one step behind the sportspeople and their chemists.

See also The World of Sport Examined Page **118-123**

© Andy Sibson Published by Thomas Nelson and Sons Ltd. 1997

Research Tasks

1. The 1991 COMA report into healthy eating found a number of problems with our diet. It also provided us with advice. List the problems that it found and present a summary of the advice that it gave.

2. Using the terms Basal Metabolic Rate (BMR) and Physical Activity Level (PAL) explain why we need energy. Discuss the importance of balancing the energy equation in your explanation.

3. Make notes about the relationship between diet and sporting performance. Refer to obesity and anorexia in your notes.

4. Using your knowledge of food types and the different demands of endurance and strength events, present dietary guidelines for endurance and strength athletes. Your guidelines should include the components of a balanced diet and examples of specific foods to be eaten.

5. Explain how our pattern of sleep and rest affects our sports performance.

6. List and explain the negative effects, on sporting performance, of smoking cigarettes and drinking alcohol.

7. Explain what drugs are and discuss the use of drugs in sport.

8. Some athletes seek ways to enhance performance that do not involve drugs. One example is blood doping. Describe this method. Explain how it works and list the dangers that accompany it.

© Andy Sibson Published by Thomas Nelson and Sons Ltd. 1997

See also The World of Sport Examined Pages **104-123**

Injury Prevention

As performers, we must take responsibility for our own safety by preparing well. We must also be alert throughout the activity itself. Complete this list of safety factors. Give five ways in which we can prepare for safety, and five ways in which we can ensure our safety during activity. One has been completed for you.

■ Preparation

1.	2. Diet and fluid	3.	4.	5.
	We need enough fuel for the activity, or we will become fatigued. We should drink little and often whilst exercising.			

■ During activity

1.	2.	3.	4.	5.

Organisers of sport also have responsibilities. They must ensure:
a) that equipment and facilities are safe; b) that rules are followed;
c) that players are matched for size.

See also The World of Sport Examined Pages **128-129**

Why do Sports Injuries Happen?

In order to avoid sports injuries, we need to know what they are
and why they happen.
Complete the diagram below by adding notes to describe each
type of injury.

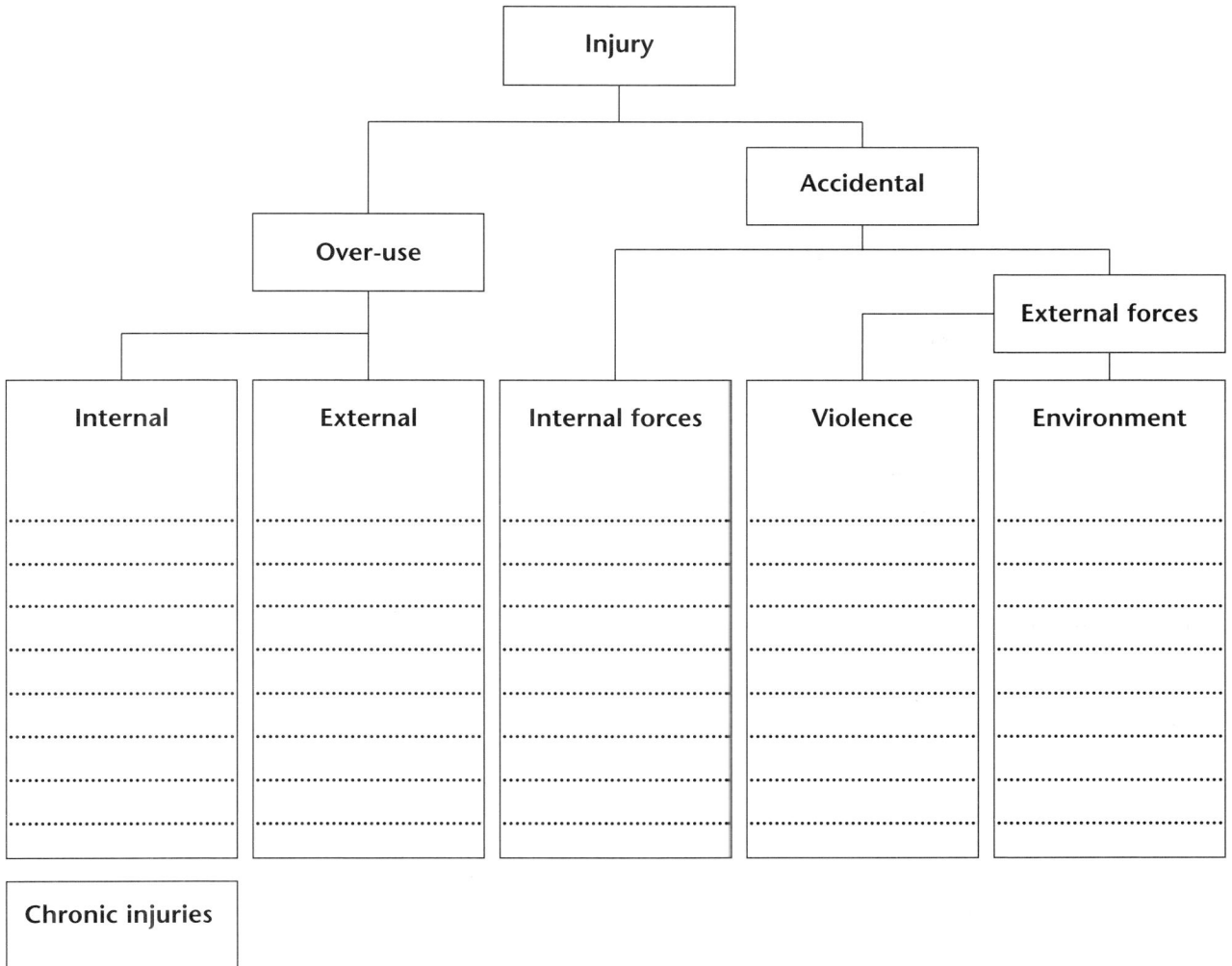

See also The World of Sport Examined Page **130**

First Aid

We often use the term 'first aid' to describe the whole of what we
do when we meet an emergency situation. Fill in the missing words below.
In an emergency we must:

1. ....
2. ....
3. ....
4. ....

If we are not sure how to deal with an injury we must ....

We must not move an injured person if ....

We must have a plan of action for any emergency. We need to
know what to do first. If someone has collapsed, remember D.R.A.B.C.
Write below left what each letter stands for.
Briefly explain, below right, what you would do at each stage.

D ....   ➡   ....

....

R ....   ➡   ....

....

A ....   ➡   ....

....

B ....   ➡   ....

....

C ....   ➡   ....

....

See also The World of Sport Examined Page **131**

© Andy Sibson Published by Thomas Nelson and Sons Ltd. 1997

Soft Tissue Injuries

Complete the sections below. Look at page 137, 'The World of Sport Examined', to help you.

Soft tissue injuries include damage to:

....
....
....
....
....

■ Types of soft tissue injury

Sprains

Sprains happen when we over-stretch or tear a ....,

for example .... We must use the

.... treatment to treat the sprains.

If the injury is severe we should treat it as a ....

Strains

Strains happen when we stretch or tear a ...., or a

.... For example .... We must

use the .... treatment to treat strains.

Cartilage (damage in the knee)

The two cartilages act as ....

between the bones of the knee joint. They can be torn by, for

example ....

We would need to seek ....

See also The World of Sport Examined Page **137**

Soft Tissue Injuries: Minor Problems

We should deal with minor soft tissue injuries quickly and carefully,
or they could become more serious.
Write down the right treatments in the spaces provided below.
The first one has been done for you.

Skin damage	Treatment
Cuts	*Clean with running water. Clean the area around the cut.* *Cover with a dressing and sticking plaster, or just a plaster.*
Grazes	
Blisters	
Other conditions	
Bruises	
Cramps	
Stitch	
Athlete's foot	
Verrucas	

See also The World of Sport Examined Page **137**

R.I.C.E. Treatment

R.I.C.E. treatment is a checklist to follow in the case of soft
tissue injury.
We can also add a P and a D to make P.R.I.C.E.D. which is a more
complete guide to injury prevention and treatment.

1. Write down the word each letter stands for, below left.
2. Explain the importance of P and D.
3. Give: (a) the reason for each stage of R.I.C.E. and (b) describe
   the action you would take.

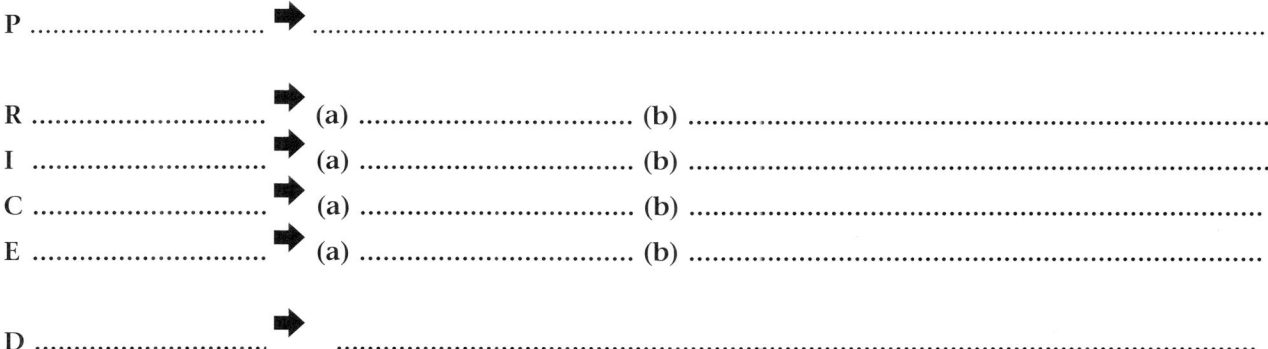

P .... ➡ ....

R .... ➡ (a) .... (b) ....
I .... ➡ (a) .... (b) ....
C .... ➡ (a) .... (b) ....
E .... ➡ (a) .... (b) ....

D .... ➡ ....

Certain things should be avoided when treating a soft tissue injury.
These are things that cause H.A.R.M.

1. Write down the word each letter stands for, below left.
2. Explain the reason why these should be avoided, below right.

H .... ➡ ....
A .... ➡ ....
R .... ➡ ....
M .... ➡ ....

See also The World of Sport Examined Pages **136-137** ➡

Fractures

■ What is a fracture?

A fracture is a break in a bone. There are two types of fracture.
1. Write a description below of each type of fracture.
2. Label the diagrams showing each type of fracture.

A closed fracture is ....
....

An open fracture is ....
....

....

■ Stress fractures

Stress fractures are small cracks in a bone. They can be caused by
too much running on hard surfaces.
1. Write down the signs that suggest a stress fracture.
2. List the things that we would need to do in the case of a stress fracture.

Signs of a stress fracture are ....
....

In the case of a stress fracture, we should:

1. ....
2. ....
3. ....
4. ....

See also The World of Sport Examined Pages **138**

Bone and Joint Injuries

Injuries to joints include fractures, dislocations and torn ligaments.

■ Dislocation

A dislocation means that a bone at a joint is forced out of its
normal range of movement. This often causes further damage.
Answer the following questions.

1. What else might be damaged when a bone is dislocated?

....

2. What might cause a dislocation?

....

3. How should dislocations be treated?

....

■ Other bone and joint injuries

We can often tell that a bone or joint injury has happened by
recognising the tell tale signs.

1. List two ways of recognising bone or joint injuries.

   a. ....

   b. ....

2. List seven signs of bone or joint injury that can be checked
   for immediately.

   a. ....

   b. ....

   c. ....

   d. ....

   e. ....

   f. ....

   g. ....

3. Describe the three actions that you would take in treating a
   bone or joint injury.

   a. ....

   b. ....

   c. ....

See also The World of Sport Examined Page **138**

Emergency Procedures

Complete the table below.

Condition	What is this condition?	What do we check for?	What action do we need to take to treat it?
Concussion			
Shock			
Hypothermia			
Heat exhaustion			
Heatstroke			
Breathing stopped			
Loss of pulse			
Serious bleeding			

See also The World of Sport Examined Pages **132-135**

Research Tasks

1. Describe and explain the principles of First Aid (or, Emergency Aid).

2. Name and describe three types of soft tissue injury.

3. Explain P.R.I.C.E.D. and H.A.R.M. in relation to soft tissue injuries.

4. Describe the treatment for minor soft tissue injuries and other minor conditions often experienced by sportspeople. Ensure that you explain how each condition occurs.

5. List four types of hard tissue injury. Explain how you would treat each one.

See also The World of Sport Examined Pages **124-139**

Revision Checklist
Tick the boxes.

■ Care of our body

Do I ...

1. ... understand what a 'balanced diet' means? ☐

2. ... know what happens if people eat too much or too little? ☐

3. ... understand how tiredness and lack of sleep will affect performance? ☐

4. ... know how important personal hygiene is to health? ☐

5. ... understand the effect of cigarettes and alcohol on performance? ☐

6. ... know which drugs some sportspeople use to aid performance? ☐

7. ... know what sports governing bodies are doing to combat drug use? ☐

Can I ...

1. ... list the seven components of a balanced diet? ☐

2. ... give examples of foods containing each component? ☐

3. ... explain the energy equation? ☐

4. ... define 'obese'? ☐

5. ... explain what type of food will help an endurance athlete? ☐

6. ... explain what type of food will help a strength athlete? ☐

7. ... explain what athlete's foot and verrucas are and how to treat them? ☐

8. ... give examples of drugs used by sportspeople and say why they are used? ☐

■ Safety in sport

Do I ...

1. ... know the principles of first aid? ☐

2. ... understand D.R.A.B.C.? ☐

3. .... understand R.I.C.E.? ☐

4. ... understand H.A.R.M.? ☐

Can I ...

1. ... list four safety factors likely to reduce the risk of injury? ☐

2. ... list two examples of soft tissue injuries and say how to treat them? ☐

3. ... describe how to treat a fracture or joint injury? ☐

4. ... list five conditions which might occur in sport, and which need emergency procedures? ☐

See also The World of Sport Examined Pages **104-139**

Revision Checklist

Tick the boxes.

■ Care of our body

Do I ...

1. ... understand what is meant by a 'balanced diet'? ☐
2. ... understand the effect of an imbalance in the diet? ☐
3. ... understand the effect of tiredness and lack of sleep on performance? ☐
4. ... know how important personal hygiene is to health? ☐
5. ... understand the effect of cigarettes and alcohol on performance? ☐
6. ... know which drugs some sportspeople use to aid performance? ☐
7. ... know what sports governing bodies are doing to combat drug use? ☐

Can I ...

1. ... list the seven components of a balanced diet? ☐
2. ... give examples of foods containing each component? ☐
3. ... explain the energy equation? ☐
4. ... define 'obese'? ☐
5. ... plan a specific diet for an endurance athlete? ☐
6. ... plan a specific diet for a strength athlete? ☐
7. ... explain what athlete's foot and verrucas are and how to treat them? ☐
8. ... list six different drugs used by sportspeople and explain their effects? ☐

■ Safety in sport

Do I ...

1. ... know the principles of first aid? ☐
2. ... understand D.R.A.B.C.? ☐
3. ... understand R.I.C.E.? ☐
4. ... understand H.A.R.M.? ☐

Can I ...

1. ... list six safety factors that are likely to reduce the risk of injury? ☐
2. ... list three examples of each type of soft tissue and explain the treatment for each? ☐
3. ... describe the treatment for a fracture or joint injury? ☐
4. ... explain the difference between an open and a closed fracture? ☐
5. ... list and describe seven conditions that might occur in sport and which need emergency procedures? ☐

See also The World of Sport Examined Pages **104-139**

Sport in Society

Competitive sport has been a feature of human life for many centuries.

When competition between villages and towns was extended to include international matches and tournaments, associations were formed to organise sport. Today the whole world plays to the same rules in most sports.

Most competitors take their sport seriously, as do the supporters, and in many countries even politicians and public figures will watch and comment on sport. Most people still participate in sport for fun, but top players can earn a lot of money. The rise of professionalism in sport has been supported by the media. Television companies pay to publicise sport and the coverage encourages sponsors to advertise their businesses through sport. The media has had both positive and negative effects on sport.

Sport has a major impact on society. The media and the population as a whole pay attention to every aspect of sport, from school P.E. lessons to world championships. Because people care about sports, so do politicians. Politicians show interest in their country's success in international sports competitions. Some Governments dictate who their country's sportspeople may compete against. In this way, politics can interfere with sport.

The Government supports sport through a number of initiatives, including the National Lottery, but there is never enough money made available to satisfy everyone.

The health benefits of sport for the whole population are widely known. Local authorities and other organisations provide sports facilities throughout the country.

Millions of people regularly play sport and many are active in trying to increase opportunities for all.

See also The World of Sport Examined Pages **140-163** and **204-219**

© Andy Sibson Published by Thomas Nelson and Sons Ltd. 1997

A Brief History of Sport

Complete this timeline by entering the major events against the year listed. The first major event has been given for you.

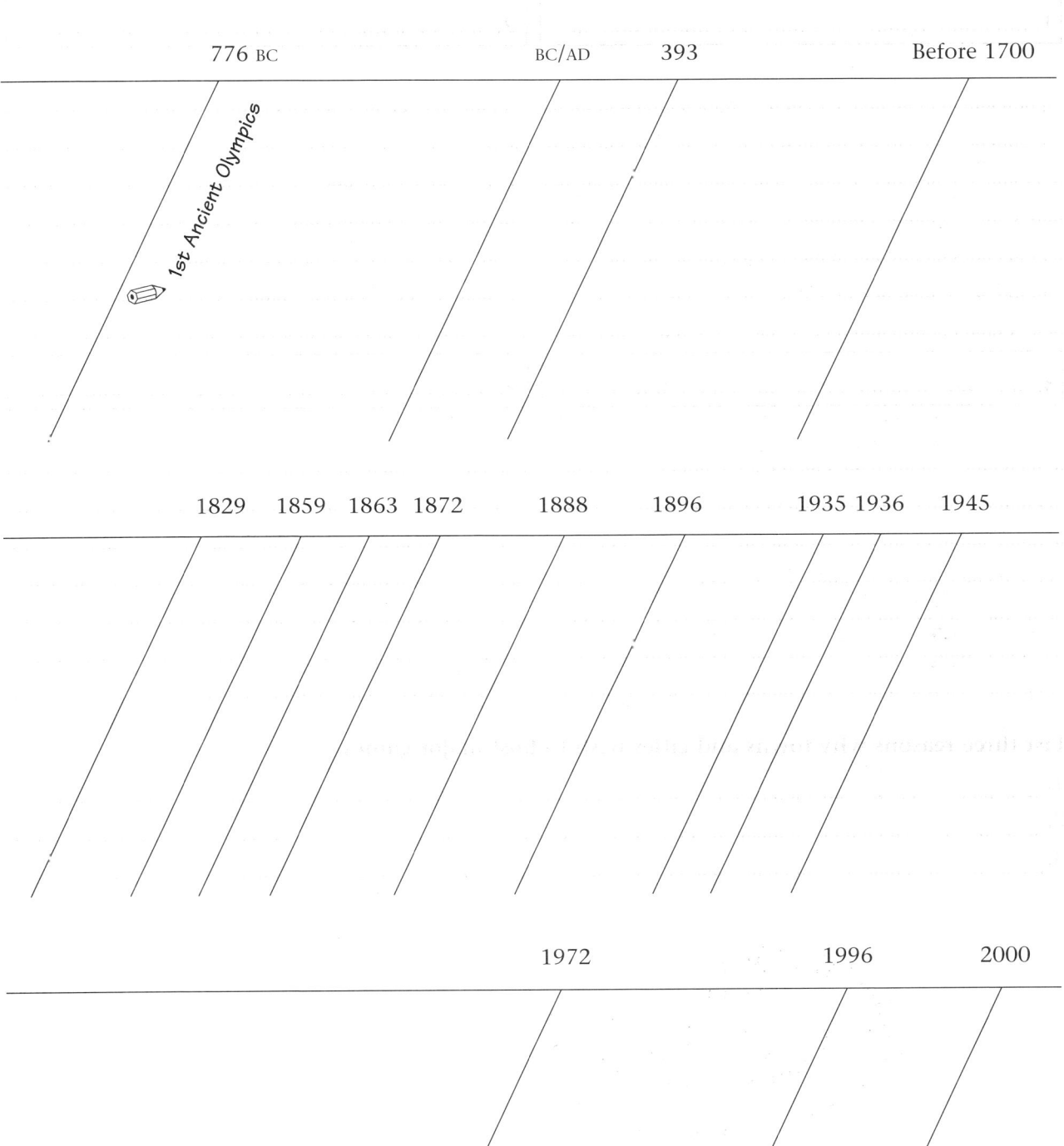

| 776 BC | | BC/AD | 393 | | Before 1700 |

1st Ancient Olympics

| 1829 | 1859 | 1863 | 1872 | 1888 | 1896 | 1935 | 1936 | 1945 |

| 1972 | | 1996 | 2000 |

Events in Olympic History

Read about the modern Olympic Games and choose four recent games to write about below. Put the date and the city in which the Olympics were held in the box and list the key events below.

1. ....

2. ....

....
....
....
....
....
....
....

3. ....

4. ....

....
....
....
....
....
....
....

List three reasons why towns and cities wish to host major games.

1. ....

2. ....

3. ....

See also The World of Sport Examined Pages **150-153**

© Andy Sibson Published by Thomas Nelson and Sons Ltd. 1997

Amateurs and Professionals

During the last 100 years, sportspeople have been labelled as 'Amateurs' or 'Professionals'. Most sports today are open. This means that no distinction is made between amateurs and professionals. Complete the following sentences.

An amateur, in sport, is ....
....
....

A professional, in sport, is ....
....
....

■ Trust funds

In the 1980s, some amateur sports created 'Trust funds' to try to help sportspeople to receive money, but remain amateur. This was a step towards professionalism for these sportspeople. Describe how trust funds worked.

....
....
....
....

■ Attitudes to sport

Read the following statements and decide which attitude applies to 'Amateurs' and which to 'Professionals'. Write 'Amateur' or 'Professional' after each statement.

1. 'Winning is all important for them.'
2. 'They are not paid.'
3. 'They must take part in competitions.'
4. 'They usually train full-time.'
5. 'They train and compete in their own time.'
6. 'No one can force them to take part.'
7. 'Sport is their work.'
8. 'Taking part is more important than the result for them.'
9. 'The more successful they are, the more money they earn.'
10. 'It is a leisure time activity for them.'

See also The World of Sport Examined Pages **156-159** 83

Being a Professional

Amateurs have less time to train and cannot reach the high
standards achieved by professional sportspeople. However, life
as a professional sportsperson has both ups and downs.
List five advantages and five disadvantages below. The first has
been given for you.

Advantages of being a professional	Disadvantages of being a professional
1. You can spend all day playing sport	1. The media can cause lots of pressure.
2.	2.
3.	3.
4.	4.
5.	5.

There are few full time professional sportspeople in the UK.
Write a list of the five sports which have the most
professional players.

1.

2.

3.

4.

5.

See also The World of Sport Examined Page **159**

Technological Development

There are five areas in which advances in technology can improve sporting performance (see below). Write about each and give examples below.

■ Machines

....

....

....

■ Clothing

....

....

....

■ Facilities

....

....

....

....

■ Training and Coaching

....

....

....

....

■ Equipment

(Include specific examples of improvement from at least two sports.)

....

....

....

....

See also The World of Sport Examined Pages **160-161** ➡

Research Tasks

1. Compare and contrast amateur and professional sportspeople. Focus on the reasons why they participate, the differences in their attitudes to sport and the advantages and disadvantages of both amateur and professional status.

2. Describe the ways in which some sportspeople were able to get around the amateur rules in the period after 1945.

3. Explain the role of the Sports Aid Foundation (S.A.F.) in aiding top performers.

4. "The 1980 Olympic Games should have been the last. They cause nothing but trouble these days. The Olympic spirit is dead." Discuss.

   Use information from the extension boxes in 'The World of Sport Examined' to support your view.

5. Advances in technology have led to great improvements in sporting performance. Which of the five areas of new technology has had the biggest influence?

See also The World of Sport Examined Pages **146-161**

Revision Checklist

Tick the boxes.

Do I ...

1. ... know that sport reflects the society in which it is found? ☐

2. ... know the difference between amateurism and professicnalism in sport? ☐

3. ... know what is meant by an 'open' sport? ☐

4. ... know what a trust fund is? ☐

5. ... know why countries like to host major sports events? ☐

Can I ...

1. ... list five sports which have the highest number of professional players in the UK? ☐

2. ... list five possible disadvantages of being a professional sportsperson? ☐

3. ... explain any disadvantages of being an amateur sportsperson? ☐

4. ... explain how amateurs and professionals have different attitudes to sport? ☐

5. ... list the major problems surrounding recent Olympic Games? ☐

6. ... give two examples of the technological development of sports equipment? ☐

See also The Wor d of Sport Examined Pages **140-163**

Revision Checklist
Tick the boxes.

Do I ...

1. ... know the difference between amateurism and professionalism in sport? ☐

2. ... know what is meant by an 'open' sport? ☐

3. ... know what a trust fund is and how it works? ☐

4. ... understand why countries choose to host major sports events? ☐

Can I ...

1. ... demonstrate how sport reflects the society in which it is found? ☐

2. ... list six sports which have the highest number of professional players in the UK? ☐

3. ... list seven possible disadvantages of being a professional sportsperson? ☐

4. ... explain any disadvantages of being an amateur sportsperson? ☐

5. ... explain the difference in attitudes to sport of amateurs and professionals? ☐

6. ... describe the major issues surrounding recent Olympic Games? ☐

7. ... give four examples of the technological development of sports equipment? ☐

See also The World of Sport Examined Pages **140-163**

Organising British Sport

Sports clubs and governing bodies are independent in the UK, although the Sports Council looks after them overall. It is the sports clubs and governing bodies who are at the heart of sport.

■ The Structure of Sport in Britain

This diagram needs to show the links between international federations and individual club members. Write the name of each organisation in its correct place in the structure below.

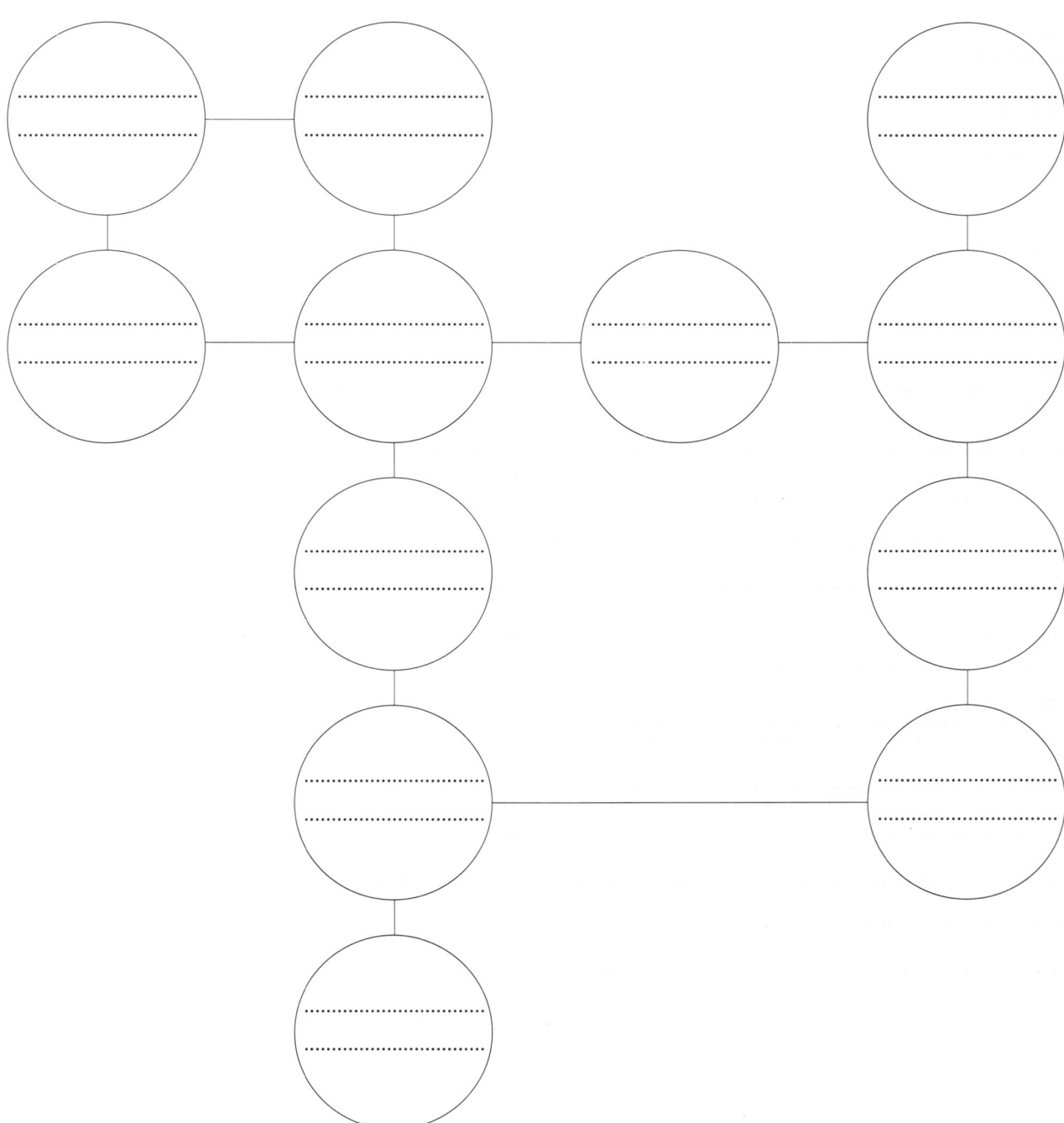

Important Organisations

The national governing bodies of sport are voluntary organisations that ensure the smooth running of each sport. They organise competitions and enforce rules. Governing bodies encourage the development of their sport. They are supported by a number of organisations or agencies.

1. Write the name of each organisation below.

2. Briefly describe each organisation.

1. ....

....

....

....

....

....

2. ....

....

....

....

....

....

3. ....

....

....

....

....

....

4. ....

....

....

....

....

....

5. ....

....

....

....

....

....

6. ....

....

....

....

....

....

See also The World of Sport Examined Pages **165-171**

© Andy Sibson Published by Thomas Nelson and Sons Ltd. 1997

Who Provides Sports Facilities?

Sports facilities are provided in three ways:
1. by the public sector;
2. by the private sector;
3. by the voluntary sector.
The private sector provides specialist facilities for the public to use
and arenas in which top players perform.
The voluntary sector includes sports clubs, community
associations and the national governing bodies.

■ The public sector

1. Complete the diagram to show the range of facilities provided
   by the government and the local authorities.

2. Write a brief explanation of dual use.

3. Write a brief explanation of joint provision.

Organising a Sports Club

Imagine that you are going to create a brand new sports club.
Complete this planning sheet to remind you of all the things
that are needed. Page 186 of 'The World of Sport Examined'
will help you.

Name of club: ....

1. Write down the titles of three essential people/roles needed. Describe what each does below.

1.	2.	3.

2. Write down the titles of the other people you need in your club. List their qualities below.

1.	2.

3. Write down three important factors to consider in setting up your club.
   Give your reasons below.

1.	2.	3.

4. Your club will need to affiliate to a regional and national association.
   Give the name, or initials, of the organiser/association at each level.

    International   National   Regional   Club

See also The World of Sport Examined Page **186**

The Sports Council

■ National campaigns

The Sports Council launched the Sport for All campaign
in 1972 and it is still going strong. It has five main aims.
Write these below.

1. ....

2. ....

3. ....

4. ....

5. ....

■ Special campaigns

At different times, the Sport for All campaign has focused on
different themes. Write these below, next to the correct date.

1975 .... 1978 ....

1981 .... 1983 ....

1985 .... 1987 ....

1990 .... 1991 ....

National campaigns can be very effective if local clubs
understand the national message and work hard to make the
campaign successful. The campaign to support sportspeople
with disabilities succeeded in providing facilities and raising
standards of performance.

■ Sport and people with disabilities

Write down three problems that sportspeople with disabilities
have to overcome.

1. .... ➡ ....

2. .... ➡ ....

3. .... ➡

The Sports Council's policy on sport and people with disabilities
has seven objectives. You decide which are the four most
important objectives and write them down.

1. .... 2. ....

3. .... 4. ....

See also The World of Sport Examined Pages **197 and 200**

Sport Participation Questionnaire

Conduct this questionnaire with two adults who play sport and two who do not.

	Player		Non-player	
	1	2	1	2
1. Did you enjoy P.E. at school?				
2. What did you like the most about P.E.?				
3. What did you dislike the most about P.E.?				
4. What were your P.E. teachers like?				
5. Did you play for your school?				
6. Did you play for a club outside school?				
7. Did your parents play sport?				
8. Do you watch sport on television?				
9. Do you think there is too much sport on television?				
10. Do you take part in physical activity other than competitive sport? If yes, what?				
11. Do you know what is available at your local sports centre?				
12. Do you use the sports centre?				
13. What is the main reason why you do/do not play sport?				
14. What is your favourite interest/hobby?				

Read pages 191-193 of 'The World of Sport Examined' and compare the responses to your questionnaire with the factors that affect participation in sport.

See also The World of Sport Examined Pages **188-189**

© Andy Sibson Published by Thomas Nelson and Sons Ltd 1997

Participation in Sport and Recreation

■ Leisure time

Complete the sentence to show what leisure time is.
Most of us play sport in our leisure time. Leisure time is ....
....

■ Reasons for taking part

We take part in sport for many different reasons.
Give four reasons why people take part in sport.

1. .... 2 ....
3. .... 4. ....

■ Influences

There are five ways in which our home affects our
participation in sport.
Name these, below left, and give examples, below right.

1. .... ➡ ....
2. .... ➡ ....
3. .... ➡ ....
4. .... ➡ ....
5. .... ➡ ....

■ Changes in P.E.

Our experiences at school are important as they influence whether
we take part in sport later in life. Five changes in education have
affected P.E. in recent years. Briefly state these changes below.

1. ....
2. ....
3. ....
4. ....
5. ....

See also The World of Sport Examined Pages **190-194** ➡

How do our P.E. lessons affect us?

Fill in the missing words. Look at page 195 of 'The World of Sport Examined', to help you.

■ Skills

P.E. teachers teach all pupils the .... of a variety of different activities. We develop these skills so that we can take part .... in the activities. Teachers may also .... these abilities through .... during after school practices. Sometimes they will send pupils to local .... or .... of .... In school we can try for .... in different sports.

■ Health

P.E. teachers explain the .... of .... exercise for .... and .... We learn .... for all activities.

■ Attitude

P.E. teachers try to develop a .... attitude towards an .... lifestyle.

■ School and community links

Even if a school's P.E. programme is very good, the link between the school and the community is vital in helping the school's young people to continue with physical recreation after they leave school. State three ways in which schools could help bridge the gap between schools and the community.

1. ....
2. ....
3. ....

State three ways in which clubs and centres could help bridge the gap between schools and the community.

1. ....
2. ....
3. ....

See also The World of Sport Examined Page **195**

A. School P.E. Survey

Find the answers to the following questions. You can answer from
your own knowledge, or ask staff and pupils in the school.

1. How many hours P.E. are done per week in the school?

KS3	KS4

2. How many sports facilities are there in the school? List the
   school's facilities on the table below, e.g. under 'Indoor courts',
   you might write:
   - four badminton
   - one volleyball
   - one basketball
     'Other facilities' includes gymnasium, table tennis, swimming
     pool, orienteering course, climbing wall, e.t.c.

Indoor courts	Outdoor courts	Pitches	Other facilities

3. How many extra curricular sports clubs are available? List the
   sports clubs under the headings below.

Girls	Boys	Mixed

See also The World of Sport Examined Pages **194-195**

B. School P.E. Survey

4. How many sports does the school compete in, with other schools?
   List these under the headings in the table below.

Girls	Boys	Mixed

5. In which sport is your school strongest?

Girls	Boys	Mixed

6. Why is this?

....

....

....

....

7. How many pupils take part in school sports clubs and teams?

....

Find out the above and then calculate below the percentage of all
pupils who are involved in sports clubs and teams.

....

8. How might this number be increased?

....

....

....

See also The World of Sport Examined Pages **194-195**

© Andy Sibson Published by Thomas Nelson and Sons Ltd. 1997

Local Facilities Survey

1a. On an outline map of your local area, mark in all of
    the sports facilities.
    These would include:
- parks and open spaces;
- sports and leisure centres;
- swimming pools;
- school halls and gymnasia;
- youth clubs' facilities;
- arenas for major events;
- golf courses;
- bowling greens;
- cricket pitches;
- hard surface areas for games.

Remember to use a key. Different colours will help.

1b. Analyse three facilities by completing the tables on the Sports
    Facilities Survey sheet.

2. Make a study of one of the facilities on your local area map.
    Find answers to the following questions.

Organisation

What are the names of the manager, assistants and coaches? Are
they full time or part time?

Membership

What is the total number of members (male and female)?
What is the age range of members?
What is the cost of membership?

Activities offered

Make a chart to show the programme run by the centre.

Finances

How is the centre funded?
What is the cost of playing each sport?
What happens to the money?

Interest groups

Are special efforts made to attract any of the following interest groups:
- women;
- the elderly;
- the disabled;
- single parent families;
- school leavers?

You must be prepared to present your findings to the class.

© Andy Sibson Published by Thomas Nelson and Sons Ltd. 1997

See also The World of Sport Examined Page **196**

Sports Facilities Survey

Analyse three sports facilities by completing this table.

Facility	Location	Condition	How could this facility be expanded, or improved?
1.			
2.			
3.			

Does your area need new facilities for any sport?

New facility needed	Location	What would this facility provide, potentially?

See also The World of Sport Examined Page **196**

© Andy Sibson Published by Thomas Nelson and Sons Ltd. 1997

Research Tasks

■ Providing for sport *See also* The World of Sport Examined Pages **164-187**

1. Research how sport is funded. Prepare a report that explains why sport needs money. List the sources of funding that are available.
2. List the organisations that receive Government money for sport.
3. Explain, in detail, how local authorities obtain money to fund sport. List the areas in which this money is spent. Do you think that they provide enough financial support for sport?
4. List the types of support that the National Lottery provides for sport. Explain the limits within which it can give grants.

■ Taking part in sport *See also* The World of Sport Examined Pages **188-203**

1. List the four types of activity that we engage in each day and explain 'leisure time' in detail.
2. Write out a table to illustrate the reasons why we take part in sport. Include information about each reason.
3. List and explain the ways in which our home circumstances affect our participation in sport.
4. Make notes about the way in which P. E. teachers and sports clubs combine to encourage participation in sport outside school.
5. Make a list of the different types of career available in the world of sport. Choose one for which you are well suited and explain why.

© Andy Sibson Published by Thomas Nelson and Sons Ltd. 1997

Revision Checklist

Tick the boxes.

■ Providing for sport

Do I ...

1. ... know the roles that have to be undertaken in a sports club? ☐

2. ... know where government money for sport comes from? ☐

3. ... know how governing bodies raise money? ☐

4. ... know what governing bodies use their money for? ☐

5. ... know that sportspeople may obtain sponsorship from the S.A.F.? ☐

Can I ...

1. ... explain how one sport is organised from local to international level? ☐

2. ... list four providers of sports facilities? ☐

3. ... list five sources of funding for sport? ☐

■ Taking part in sport

Do I ...

1. ... know what is meant by 'leisure time'? ☐

2. ... know what is meant by 'recreation'? ☐

3. ... understand the importance of school P.E.? ☐

4. ... know how schools and communities link to provide sport for all? ☐

5. ... know what influences people to play sport after they leave school? ☐

6. ... know what special provision is made for disabled people? ☐

Can I ...

1. ... list four reasons for taking part in sport? ☐

2. ... name six agencies who organise and support sport and recreation? ☐

3. ... describe what each agency does? ☐

4. ... describe a Government policy to improve sport? ☐

See also The World of Sport Examined Pages **164-203**

© Andy Sibson Published by Thomas Nelson and Sons Ltd. 1997

Revision Checklist
Tick the boxes.

■ Providing for sport

Do I ...
1. ... understand the roles undertaken within a successful sports club? ☐
2. ... know the role of the S.A.F.? ☐
3. ... know where Government money for sport comes from? ☐
4. ... know how governing bodies raise money? ☐
5. ... know what governing bodies use their money for? ☐

Can I ...
1. ... list eight sources of funding for sport? ☐
2. ... list four providers of sports facilities? ☐

■ Taking part in sport

Do I ...
1. ... know what is meant by the term 'leisure time'? ☐
2. ... understand what is meant by the term 'recreation'? ☐
3. ... understand the importance of school P.E. in influencing participation? ☐
4. ... know how schools and communities link to provide sport for all? ☐
5. ... know what influences people to play sport after they leave school? ☐
6. ... know what special provision is made for disabled people? ☐

Can I ...
1. ... list four reasons for taking part in sport? ☐
2. ... name seven agencies responsible for organising sport and recreation? ☐
3. ... explain what each agency is responsible for? ☐
4. ... explain how one sport is organised from local to international level? ☐
5. ... describe two government initiatives designed to improve sport? ☐

See also The World of Sport Examined Pages **164-203** ➡

What is Sports Sponsorship?

Complete the sentence below.

Sports sponsorship means that a .... gives financial help in return for

.... its name with an ...., a ....

or a .... in general.

■ Why do companies sponsor sport?

List four advantages of sponsorship for the sponsor.

1. ....

2. ....

3. ....

4. ....

■ Why does sport like sponsorship?

List four advantages of sponsorship for the sport.

1. ....

2. ....

3. ....

4. ....

■ What problems does sponsorship create?

List four disadvantages of sponsorship for the sport.

1. ....

2. ....

3. ....

4. ....

5. ....

List four disadvantages of sponsorship for the sponsor.

1. ....

2. ....

3. ....

4. ....

5. ....

■ The S.A.F.

The Sports Aid Foundation (S.A.F.) provides an important source
of funds for individual players. It is paid for by sponsoring
companies and donations.

List four ways in which the S.A.F. helps players.

1. ....

2. ....

3. ....

4. ....

See also The World of Sport Examined Pages **206-211**

© Andy Sibson Published by Thomas Nelson and Sons Ltd 1997

Sponsorship and the Media

1. Watch television and read newspapers during one weekend.
   List all the sponsors that you see (do not include advertising
   hoardings) below. In the third column, write down the form
   of the sponsorship, e.g. was it sponsoring a club? Was it shown
   on a shirt, or in the title of an event? Did you see it on the
   television or in a newspaper?

Sponsor name	Sport	Form of sponsorship

2. List six major events and the sponsors of those events.

Sponsor name	Event
1.	
2.	
3.	
4.	
5.	
6.	

See also The World of Sport Examined Pages **206-213**

Sport on Television

■ The Media

When we talk about the media, we are referring to all the different ways that are used to bring us stories and news. There are five main types of media. List them below.

1. .... 2. ....

3. .... 4. ....

5. ....

■ How is sport shown on television?

Sport on television appears in many different forms. We can watch .... as they take place and then see the edited .... later. .... programmes bring the results of major events. Sports .... documentaries and .... programmes are also popular. Television also supplies sports information throughout the day and night on .... and ....

■ Who controls what we watch?

Many decisions about what we watch are made by television companies and sponsors in their own interests rather than in the interests of the sport itself.

■ What are the benefits of televising sport?

List three benefits for sport of televising sport.

1. ....

2. ....

3. ....

■ What problems does television coverage create?

List three problems which television coverage causes for sport.

1. ....

2. ....

3. ....

See also The World of Sport Examined Pages **212-216**

© Andy Sibson Published by Thomas Nelson and Sons Ltd 1997

The Image of Sport

**Newspapers and television play a major part in forming
our views about sport.**

■ Newspapers

Draw arrows to match the words below.

The aim of editors is ...   •   • ... knocking them down.

Some newspapers carry more details about ... •   • ... building up stars.

Newspapers are good at ...   •   • ... affects how we think about sport.

However, they are even better at ...   •   • ... to sell more newspapers.

The way that sportswriters present sport ... •   • ... the private lives of the sports stars than
                                                                                            about the sport itself.

■ Television

**The way that sport is presented on television affects our own views
in a similar way to the newspapers. It can reinforce stereotypes by
presenting certain images and ignoring others.
Draw arrows to match the words below.**

'So called' experts may ...   •   • ... older people, people with disabilities
                                                                                            and women.

We must remember that ...   •   • ... praise a particular player.

In the past, sport on television was ...   •   • ... the appearance of sportswomen.

Today we often see ...   •   • ... these are only opinions.

However, commentators still comment on ... •   • ... dominated by young, able-bodied males.

See also The World of Sport Examined Pages **212-216**

A Terrestrial and Satellite Television Survey

1. Conduct a survey of the terrestrial and satellite television coverage of sport during one week (you can use a television listings magazine to help you). Complete the table below.

Terrestrial television (TTV)		Satellite television	
Live coverage	Hours	Live coverage	Hours
Total number of sports	**Total hours**	**Total number of sports**	**Total hours**
Recorded highlights	Hours	Recorded highlights	Hours
Total sports	**Total hours**	**Total sports**	**Total hours**

2. Compare the number of sports covered by terrestrial and satellite television.

a. Which covered the most 'minority' sports?

....

b. Which covered more women's events?

....

c. Why might this be?

....

d. What problems does this create for women's sport?

....

....

See also The World of Sport Examined Page **214**

© Andy Sibson Published by Thomas Nelson and Sons Ltd. 1997

Comparing Newspapers

1. Compare the sports coverage of two newspapers bought on the same day. One should be a tabloid (e.g. The Sun) and one should be a broadsheet (e.g. The Independent).
2. Complete the table below.

Tabloid name:		Broadsheet name:	
Sports covered in order of amount of coverage given.		Sports covered in order of amount of coverage given.	
1.	2.	1.	2.
3.	4.	3.	4.
5.	6.	5.	6.
7.	8.	7.	8.
9.	10.	9.	10.
11.	12.	11.	12.
13.	14.	13.	14.
15.	16.	15.	16.
17.	18.	17.	18.
19.	20.	19.	20.
21.	22.	21.	22.
23.	24.	23.	24.

Analysis

3. Which sport is given the most coverage?

Tabloid .... Broadsheet ....

4. Is the coverage mostly fact or opinion?

Tabloid .... Broadsheet ....

5. Compare the size of headlines used in each paper. What is the difference?

....

6. What effect do you think that the larger headlines have?

....

7. Which type of newspaper focuses most on famous sports personalities, or 'stars'?

....

8. How are 'stars' created? ....

Comparing newspapers and television

9. Do television and newspapers favour the same sports? ....

10. Is the amount of coverage each gives to women similar? ....

11. Where would you look for factual information about many sports? ....

12. If you wanted to be entertained, which form of coverage would you choose?

....

Research Tasks

■ The media *See also* The World of Sport Examined Pages **212-218**

1. Define 'the media' and list five forms of media in which sport is presented.
2. List and describe the different ways in which sport is presented.
3. Television coverage brings benefits to sport, but also creates problems. List and explain three benefits and three problems.
4. The opinions that we have about sport are influenced by a number of people in the newspapers and on television. Give examples of the people who influence the way that we see sport and how we think about it.
5. Why is the role of these people so important to us all?

■ Sponsorship *See also* The World of Sport Examined Pages **206-211**

1. What do we mean by 'sports sponsorship'?
2. What is the key difference between a donation and sponsorship?
3. How does a company decide which events to sponsor?
4. List the advantages and disadvantages of sponsorship for the sport.
5. List the advantages and disadvantages of sponsorship for the sponsor.
6. What are the advantages and disadvantages of sponsorship for the individual performer?
7. Where can individual sportspeople obtain sponsorship?

Revision Checklist
Tick the boxes.

Do I ...

1. ... know who decides what the public see on television? ☐

2. ... understand how the media creates 'stars'? ☐

3. ... know how sponsorship, sport and the media are linked? ☐

4. ... know how the media is used for educational purposes? ☐

5. ... understand the influence of satellite television on sport? ☐

6. ... know what the effects of sponsorship are on events, and their dates and timings? ☐

7. ... know how sportspeople can obtain sponsorship? ☐

Can I ...

1. ... list five forms of media which present sport? ☐

2. ... list three different forms of media coverage? ☐

3. ... list three advantages of media coverage? ☐

4. ... list three disadvantages of media coverage? ☐

5. ... describe the difference between the coverage of men's and women's sport? ☐

6. ... list some advantages and disadvantages of sponsorship to:

   the sponsor? ☐

   the performer? ☐

   the sport? ☐

7. ... list five major events and their sponsors? ☐

See also The Wor d of Sport Examined Pages **204-219**

Revision Checklist

Tick the boxes.

Do I ...

1. ... understand how television companies influence what the public see? ☐

2. ... understand the role of the media in creating 'stars'? ☐

3. ... understand the relationship between sponsorship, sport and the media? ☐

4. ... know how the media is used for educational purposes? ☐

5. ... understand the influence of satellite television on sport? ☐

6. ... know what the effects of sponsorship are on events, and their dates and timings? ☐

Can I ...

1. ... list five forms of media which present sport? ☐

2. ... list three different types of media coverage? ☐

3. ... list and explain five positive effects of the media coverage of sport? ☐

4. ... list and explain five negative effects of the media coverage of sport? ☐

5. ... use examples to illustrate the difference between the coverage of men's and women's sport? ☐

6. ... list the advantages and disadvantages of sponsorship to:

   the sponsor? ☐

   the performer? ☐

   the sport? ☐

7. ... list six major events and their sponsors? ☐

See also The World of Sport Examined Pages **204-219** ➡

© Andy Sibson. Published by Thomas Nelson and Sons Ltd. 1997